SELLING
WITHOUT
BUT

THE ULTIMATE GUIDE TO
OVERCOMING SALES OBJECTIONS

CW00552222

ROMAN KMENTA

Imprint

© 2023 Roman Kmenta, Forstnergasse 1, A-2540 Bad Vöslau - www.romankmenta.com

1st edition 03/2023

Cover design: Monika Stern / sternloscreative
Layout: VoV media
Illustration: VoV media
Editing/proofreading: VoV media
Image copyright: Freepik hole-from-ball 73
Publisher: VoV media - www.voice-of-value.com

ISBN Softcover: 978-3-903845-52-7
ISBN Hardcover: 978-3-903845-53-4

The contents of this book have been prepared with the greatest care. However, we cannot guarantee the accuracy, completeness and timeliness of the content. This book contains links to external websites of third parties, on whose contents we have no influence. Therefore, we cannot assume any liability for these external contents. The respective operator or provider of the pages in question is always responsible for the content of the linked pages. At the time of publication of this book, we had - after checking these websites - no indications of legal violations. Should such become known at a later date, we will remove the links as quickly as possible.

In the reproduction of common names, trade names, product designations and registered trademarks, the trademarks have been omitted - for the sake of easier readability.

The book refers to various products, some of which are available for purchase on Amazon.

TABLE OF CONTENTS

FOREWORD

As I sit across from the head of training at a prominent telecom provider, I can feel the positive energy in the air. Our relationship is strong, and we both seem to enjoy each other's company. During our conversation, I've been highlighting the exceptional training modules and content that our company has to offer. I also emphasized our wealth of experience and numerous satisfied customers as references. To further strengthen our value proposition, I mentioned that we partner with another renowned training provider, known as X.

The conversation has been going smoothly, and the head of training seems impressed with what we have to offer. Of course, the topic of pricing inevitably came up. I informed her that our prices are competitive, with rates that are in the top ten percent of the market. To my surprise, she nonchalantly mentioned that she was not surprised, given that X is also a partner of ours. X is known not just for its reputation but also for its premium pricing.

An objection, I think, and begin to refute it quite automatically and without thinking for even a second. *"Yes, but in return you also .... blah, blah, blah."* I defend my high price, justify it and myself for daring to ask so much.

She listens to me and after what feels like an eternity says, *"But that doesn't mean we wouldn't book you because of that."* This statement hits me like a slap in the face and snaps me out of my "yeah, but" trance. *"Right,"* I think, *"that doesn't mean that."*

Uncover the lessons of a lasting sales experience! This episode from two decades ago may have taken place a long time ago, but its impact remains. Did I take away anything valuable from it? Absolutely. Am I perfect in handling objections now? Not by a long shot. But, at least I can recognize my mistakes now, instead of having them pointed out by others, as in that example. These lessons are worth sharing, and that's why I wrote this book.

The mistake I made is all too common among salespeople today. That's why this book is so relevant. We'll dive deep into what went wrong and uncover hidden insights from a sales psychology perspective. Get ready to be amazed.

Objections, the normal case

Objections are a common occurrence in sales and happen more often than one might think. Whenever a customer doesn't buy, there's likely to be an objection. Even when a customer does make a purchase, there may still be objections that went unresolved. In short, objections are a constant presence in the sales process.

However, it's not always easy to recognize objections. Sometimes they are expressed loudly, other times they are whispered so quietly that they are easily missed. Customers may voice objections that are not the real ones, or keep them to themselves. Regardless of how objections are communicated, they are always present in sales interactions.

Given the prevalence of objections in sales, it's worth dedicating an entire book to this topic. Understanding objections and learning how to effectively handle them is crucial for success in sales.

Furthermore, objections are not only ubiquitous, but are often perceived as unpleasant and annoying by us salespeople. It's understandable. Of course, we'd prefer if the customer just said "Yes, I do" or signed the offer. This also occurs, but the road to the deal is frequently paved with objections.

So it's time to make friends with them, or at the very least make a truce for the duration of the book. Only then will you be able to fully absorb what I have to say on the following pages and successfully implement it in your customer meetings.

Much of what you think you know about objections is false or can be viewed from entirely different perspectives. You'll realize that you've frequently made your sales conversations unnecessarily difficult in some ways, and that they'll be much easier for you in the future. And you might even come to appreciate, even love, objections. It's possible that in the future, you'll be eager to hear your customer's next objection.

However, you will find it easier to deal with objections in any case. You will learn to deal with them in a relaxed manner because you will have many variants and strategies for dealing with such situations.

Are you curious now? So let us get started. Have a good time reading.

WHY OBJECTIONS ARE GOOD

Imagine you are talking to a customer and presenting yourself at the top of your lungs. In response to questions such as *"How do you like it?"* your customer replies with a restrained and unemotional *"Yes, quite well.* Now you might think: so far, so good. But somehow, an unpleasant feeling spreads in the pit of your stomach. Something is wrong there. Something your customer doesn't want to tell you. You don't really believe his *"Yes, quite well"*. His body language and the way he says it don't emphasize the *"Yes, quite well"*.

Not one to give up easily, you bravely ask, "Is there anything bothering you about this?" The customer gives a curt "No." Undeterred, you follow up with, "Do you have any questions?" to which the customer replies, "No, none so far." The interaction continues in this stiff manner, until the customer ultimately bids you farewell with a "I'll think about it."

Although hope springs eternal, your prospects at this point don't look too promising. You say goodbye, unsure if you'll hear from this customer again.

After you are a sales professional, you do follow up a few more times and even reach out to that customer again - on the first follow-up attempt ... then you don't.

What went wrong? The customer had said that he liked it. Okay, his words were *"quite good"*, which does not mean an intensification of the word "good" at least in my linguistic region. And yet, when asked if something was bothering him, he gave a clear "no". Nevertheless, you knew that the conversation had taken a wrong turn somewhere and then gone awry. It was perfectly clear to you from a certain moment that nothing sensible would come out of it. You have a sixth sense for this kind of thing, which you trust, no matter what the other five senses say.

It's not the voiced objections that trouble us as salespeople, but those that our customers don't voice. They are the ones they keep to themselves - for whatever reason. The ones we, therefore, don't know but can only assume. The ones that let us run into the void.

In contrast, a well-articulated objection is a valuable gift from the customer. Regardless of the outcome, whether it leads to a successful business deal or not, the customer's willingness to voice their concerns is a positive step forward. With their objections clearly stated, you have the opportunity to address and overcome any roadblocks. This openness from the customer allows for a more transparent and productive discussion, leading to a greater chance of securing the deal.

Even if you are unable to overcome an objection and the customer ultimately decides not to proceed with the deal, there is a silver lining. This situation can serve as an opportunity for growth and improvement in your product or service. If multiple customers raise the same objection, it may be a sign that there is room for improvement in that area. Although it may be disappointing in the moment, taking the time to listen to and understand your customer's objections can lead to positive changes and ultimately lead to better outcomes in the future.

"Objections are
free business consultants."

Therefore, learn to appreciate your customer's objections and see them as hurdles that you can grow from - always assuming that the customer also tells you about them. But what if they don't. What if your customer prefers to keep his objection to himself. There are ways and means by which you might be able to elicit your customer's secrets - not always, but time and again ... at least. How do you do that? We will deal with that a little later in the book.

Before we turn to such conversational methods and details, there are a few other things to do to lay the groundwork for successful conversation. For example, there are some myths that I would like to dispel.

THE 5 MOST COMMON
MYTHS ABOUT OBJECTIONS

Myths exist in all areas of life. They are ideas that are very widespread, believed to be true and therefore hardly ever questioned. But on closer inspection and analysis, the squeaky-clean facade of many a myth begins to crumble. Not everywhere, but in many places, another, perhaps its true face, is revealed behind it.

The same applies to myths concerning objections. Not that there isn't some truth to it. It's not that the myth doesn't also apply in one conversation or another. But there are many cases in which it is false and rather the opposite of true.

Myth #1: Objections are bad

I have already dispelled the myth that objections are bad. Objections are good - as explained earlier - as long as they are voiced. The only obstructions are those that you have not yet been able to elicit from the customer. But we will take care of those as well.

> *"You should be concerned if your customer does not express any objections."*

Going one step further, a lack of objections from a customer may actually be cause for concern. If a customer does not raise any objections, it could mean that they either see the offer as too good to be true or they are not fully engaged in the conversation. Either way, if there are no objections, it's a sign that you need to pay close attention. A truly sensational offer, presented in an engaging and convincing way, should inspire questions and prompt the customer to ask for more information. If this isn't happening, it's a red flag that something may not be right. Trust us, you'll know.

Or it means - and this is much more often the case - that he has an objection that he would rather still keep to himself. So you could rephrase the myth into a much truer statement: Unspoken objections are bad. I would agree with that.

Myth #2: Objections must be addressed

Only recently, I had a participant in a seminar who, in practice conversations, reacted to customer objections completely automatically and with a short and unemotional "Exactly" and then either remained silent or simply continued talking. There was no trace of objection handling.

With the casualness with which he brought the "Exactly", it would not even be interpreted as agreement. Rather, it was a rhetorical phrase that helped to overcome the customer's objection. At the same time, however, the objection was not simply ignored, but was definitely noticed and acknowledged, but without attaching too much importance to it.

And this is often the case when a customer raises an objection: the salesperson gives the objection far too much attention and weight. This exacerbates the problem that the customer has brought to the table. Frequently, they are much larger than necessary.

Of course, the type of objection and the manner in which it is raised will affect the response. Some objections cannot be brushed aside with a simple "Exactly" and some objections may be best left unaddressed. However, it is a common misconception that objections must always be "dealt with." This notion is simply not true and should be recognized as a myth. Instead, it is more important to approach each objection with thoughtful consideration and determine the best course of action based on the specific situation.

In the methods of handling objections, we will go into more detail about which objections you can safely ignore or simply perceive without reacting to them, let alone "handling" them. And there, you will also learn how to do this elegantly. Exactly.

Myth #3: Objections must be eliminated

Another myth is that objections must always be "eliminated" or "resolved." This idea is too limiting and oversimplified. It's common for consumers to make purchases despite having objections about certain aspects of the product or service. If you've ever purchased something with both pros and cons, you understand this concept. These objections, whether expressed or unspoken, are simply part of the decision-making process. As long as the customer ultimately decides to proceed with the purchase, it's all good. So, let's grant your customers the same right and allow them to have their objections. It's all part of the process.

Myth #4: Objections must be handled by the seller

Wait a minute, didn't we already have this myth? Not quite. This fourth myth is about WHO takes care of the objection. It says that, of course, and as a matter of course, it has to be the salesperson. After all, the customer brings the objection. That the salesperson then takes care of it is only fair in the sense of a balanced distribution of roles. But fair or not, it is not set in stone.

For some readers, the idea of giving the customer the task of handling objections may seem strange. But this approach definitely has advantages for you as a salesperson. Apart from having less work to do and not having the entire burden of getting the hurdles out of the way on your shoulders, answers to objections that the customer gives himself are much more convincing for him.

Why should he do that or get your customers to do that? We will deal with this in detail later on. At this point, it should be noted that the magic formula is to ask questions.

Myth #5: The seller must bring counterarguments

The magic formula just mentioned also holds the key to the fifth myth. This is based on the following, quite understandable idea: The customer brings an objection into play. He often expresses this as an argument such as *"I see this point quite differently ..."* or also as an apparent question such as *"Isn't it the case that ..."* which, however, on closer inspection represents nothing more than a veiled argument.

Challenged in this way, many salespeople readily take up the gauntlet thrown down to them and counter this argument in turn with a counter-argument. Of course, it must be one that weighs at least as heavily as that of the customer. The intention behind this is to prove to the customer that what he is saying is wrong. From here on, it's no longer about driving the sales process forward and bringing it to a happy end, but often just about being right.

And yes, if you have good arguments as a salesperson, you may succeed. You may even be able to prove that the customer is wrong using figures, data, and facts that are watertight. You may even be pleased to have won this small victory. And maybe it shows on your face, even though you don't want to let on, of course.

How does your customer react? If he has even a little bit of backbone, he will not give in so quickly and will bring another, stronger argument or, in the absence of a better one, will simply insist on his point of view. Of course, as a salesperson, you can't let this sit on your hands either and ... At some point, both of you are so deeply entrenched in your respective positions that you can no longer move toward the other. Not even if you want to.

If you are right in this little skirmish, which can also develop into a full-blown battle ... Then who is wrong? Who has lost if you win? How does the loser feel and - above all - what feelings does he have towards you? And what will the loser probably not do if he feels the way he does - and certainly not with someone like you?

"Do you want to be right or successful?"

"But don't I have to refute false statements made by the customer?" you may now be legitimately asking yourself. No, not necessarily. It depends on what effects these false statements by the customer have. If important legal or safety issues are involved, for example, they will have to be corrected at some point. But this can also be done much more elegantly than with the sledgehammer method of a counterargument.

But from my experience, most objections from a customer are not of this kind. Rather, they are ones that can be left untouched from a point of view. Those that neither concern legal or safety framework conditions nor stand in the way of closing the sale. The only thing that stands in the way is your ego as a salesperson.

You can decide if you are right or if you would rather sell something. It is your decision. You have to live with the consequences. For my part, I know what I choose, even if - I admit - it's not always easy.

THE MOST COMMON MISTAKES WHEN DEALING WITH OBJECTIONS

The most frequent errors I observe in sales practices regarding objections stem from the misconceptions previously discussed. Although there may be some overlap, I will still summarize these errors for the purpose of highlighting their significance. I believe that avoiding these errors is crucial for a successful sales pitch and a positive customer relationship. Additionally, I aim to provide practical examples and explanations to better illustrate these mistakes. The underlying factor for these errors is often the ego of the salesperson. Regardless, their importance cannot be ignored.

I admit that the following errors cannot be neatly separated from one another and stem from the same source - the salesperson's ego. However, this does not diminish their significance in the success of a sales presentation and the customer relationship in general.

React too quickly

Responding immediately to a customer's objection is one of the most basic things you can do wrong when dealing with customer objections. In fact, it's often the case that salespeople don't even wait until the objection has completely left the customer's mouth. Too often, they've already heard it and know - or rather, think they know - what's to follow. Based on their experience, they are probably often right. Sometimes, however, they are not and the customer ends the objection differently than the salesperson assumed. Most of the time, it is precisely the last words that still contain relevant information.

But aside from the information you might miss, it's just plain rude to cut someone off and not let them finish. And that's not even the worst of it. If you respond in the second, then you are being rushed. The customer drives you on with his objections. In this way, as a salesperson, you relinquish some control and lose it altogether if you're not careful. Under no circumstances should you allow this to happen.

There is no reason to respond so quickly when the customer brings an objection. Allow yourself time to fully absorb and digest the objection. For a few breaths, or a few seconds, your response may be delayed in any case. A few valuable seconds to sort through your thoughts and search for the appropriate response. The better prepared you are, the easier the search will be.

"Look smart and keep breathing."

That was the advice of one of my teachers for dealing with unexpected or challenging situations. It's not a bad idea at all, even in the face of customer objections. "Looking smart" helps you maintain the impression that you are in complete control of the situation and, of course, have an appropriate response to the customer's statement or question. Continuing to breathe gives you a little time and - also quite helpful in sales talks in general - oxygen.

Keep in mind that in extreme cases, the response to an objection can take hours or even days. For example, a customer's request for a special version (formulated as an objection: *"Well, I certainly won't buy that in this color. It doesn't match the rest of the living room at all"*) must first be clarified with the production department. Every customer will understand that this takes some time.

So put on the brakes a little and resist the impulse to have to respond immediately to an objection. You don't have to.

Discuss with customers

Avoid getting into confrontations with customers during a sales talk. This can easily escalate into arguments and cause irreparable damage to the relationship. Instead, try to diffuse any heated discussion and keep the focus on finding a solution. Both parties can leave feeling unsatisfied if a disagreement occurs. It's never a good outcome when one person leaves feeling defeated, and it's even worse if it's the customer.

Badmouthing your customer's opinions and points of view

No matter what the customer says, no matter how much it disagrees with you and your worldview, don't belittle his views. Take it for what it is: his view of the world. Of course, yours is the more correct one ... within the framework of your view of the world. By that, I don't mean agreeing with the customer and saying "yes and amen" to everything. That is not even necessary.

Rather, a lot is already done if you understand your customer's point of view without making it your own. In most cases, that's quite enough.

And if it should become quite extreme? If it's one of those statements that you just can't take note of? One of those very, very rare views where even understanding it is an impossible task? Then you have a choice: out with it and potentially do without that customer, or think whatever you want about it, but at least keep your mouth shut.

Certain words and phrases

Let's focus on certain words and phrases that are frequently encountered in connection with unproductive approaches to objection handling. They are the form in words of what has been explained in the previous paragraphs. They are so universal that they can be found in every industry, with every product and every service.

Avoid:

- **"Yes, but ..."**
  Through the "but" the pseudo agreement, which is supposed to be the "yes", is nullified and turned into the opposite. "But" at this point means that what was said before it is not true. It is the perfect introduction to an "argument-counterargument duel."

  If you must use this type of wording, use an "and" instead of the "but". "But" separates, "and" connects. "Yes and ..." supports the "yes" and makes it a sincere, honest, genuine "yes."

At the same time, "And" leaves you the opportunity to add to or expand upon the customer's viewpoint. Instead of "either/or", it's about "and/and".

There is, however, a very effective variant for using the "Yes, but ..." and achieving something very positive for you as a salesperson, your offer, and thus the sales pitch. This is explained in detail in the chapter on anticipating objections.

- ***"But you must ..."***
  Your customer doesn't have to do anything, and certainly not what you are trying to tell him to do with this kind of wording. Resist the attempt to impose rules on your customer in this way. It is all too easy to feel restricted and patronized by regulations. Who likes that? I don't. Do you?

  "Pre-suggestions instead of pre-scripts".

  Proposals are much better here than regulations. With suggestions, the customer can choose. Give him the choice. If you do it cleverly (we will get to that), he will choose in your sense.

- ***"You must not ..."***
  This formulation is the twin brother of the previous one. Instead of telling the customer what he must do, you try to tell him what he must not do with this formulation. In the end, it amounts to the same thing. The risk that your customer will go into resistance and try to take back or defend the decision-making leeway

that you want to take away from him (referred to in psychology as reactance) increases.

- ***"You can't put it that way."***
  This formulation is also in the same vein. You are trying to tell your customer what to do, which - as already mentioned - is not a very good idea in a sales conversation.

- ***"Well, I've never heard that before."***
  If this statement were an almost reverential acknowledgement of a thought expressed by your customer, then there would be nothing wrong with making such a statement. In the vast majority of cases, however, that is not the ulterior motive. Rather, it is a devaluation of what the customer has said. With the appropriate facial expressions and a tone of voice that underscores this, it's as if you were prefacing it with *"Well, what kind of nonsense is that?"* - and the customer understands it that way.

- ***"But in return, you also have ..."***
  This formulation arises from a different mental background. The salesperson feels weak or is of the opinion that his product or service is not good enough. Therefore, he begins to defend and justify his offer. *"But for that you also have ..."* is the spoken entry into such a justification. And justifying or defending his offer weakens it even more. Good products and services do not need such a thing. They are self-confident and can stand on their own two feet. They don't need a salesperson to come to their defense.

All these formulations will not always lead to disaster. If your relationship with the customer is strong and good enough, it can withstand the odd "Yes, but ..." or "You must not ...". However, these formulations are not helpful. In the better case, they undermine customer relations and the discussion climate bit by bit. In the worst case, they quickly lead to the end and the inglorious end of the sales talk.

Talk too much

Talking a lot is fully in line with the image that large parts of the population have of salespeople. Even if they are looked at a little askance for this, it is widely agreed that one of the qualities of a good salesperson is to be able to talk well and to do so often.

Incidentally, this is a myth that does not relate specifically to dealing with objections, but to sales in general. The fact is that good and, above all, successful salespeople can talk, but they are also very good at asking questions and listening. Unfortunately, when it comes to dealing with customer objections, the widespread cliché of the salesperson who talks a lot all too often comes through. Lacking other strategies and following a natural impulse, salespeople often try to meet an objection by talking it down and verbally stomping on it until it stops moving. But objections are sometimes tenacious and can't be resolved in this way.

Want to be right

That brings us back to the ego. Wanting to be right - in whatever form - is a bad idea when dealing with objections in customer discussions and in interpersonal contact in general. It quickly creates the image of a know-it-all, a smart aleck who lectures others from on high and thinks he's got the wisdom of the spoon. And that's not how you should want to come across as a salesperson.

Take it personally

Avoid taking customer objections personally. As salespeople, it's natural to be passionate about our products, services, and even our company, but it's important to remember that objections from customers are not personal attacks. This tendency can be even stronger for service providers who perform the services they are advertising, but taking customer objections as criticism can quickly lead to hurt feelings and damaged relationships.

And when we feel attacked in this way, we go into defense or counterattack. Both behaviors are not helpful and lead to the conversation going in the wrong direction.

Standing behind your company, its product, or its services is certainly good and important. Nevertheless, you should be able to retreat to the neutral standpoint of an observer in the event of an objection. From there, you can take the right next steps with less emotion and more understanding.

Do any of the listed errors sound familiar to you? Could it be that it has also happened to you once or several times? I would be surprised if not, since these behaviors are only human. But if you catch yourself doing it, even after you have committed one of these sins, don't be too hard on yourself. Why should you? You are one important step ahead. These mistakes are especially bad when you make them but don't realize it. As soon as you notice them - but only then - you can do something about them and change your behavior. Rejoice and work on changing your reactions to objections.

THE MOST COMMON OBJECTIONS

What's interesting is that - when you take a closer look - there aren't that many different objections. No matter what industry you're in and what you sell, you probably won't hear more than five to ten objections on a regular basis, if that. These will probably cover more than 90 percent of all customer objections with you.

The good news is: you know what objections your customers can or will bring. If you know these in advance, then you can prepare for them. And that's exactly what you should do. Dealing with objections should not be left to your spontaneous creative inspiration (which reliably fails to materialize in stressful situations) and certainly not to chance.

Well prepared, it should hardly ever happen that a customer surprises you with an objection. Whatever the customer says, you know how you will deal with it and have the appropriate response ready.

But you are not the only one who regularly repeats objections. Even across industries, a number of objections can be found almost everywhere in (almost) the same form, some even with the same background. What are they?

Widespread are objections to:

- **Prices**
  The clear number one in very many industries.

- **Quality**
  This objection does not always arise at the time of purchase, but rather in the context of a complaint after the customer has already used or consumed the product or service.

- **Availability/Delivery times**

- **Image**
  The image and reputation enjoyed by the seller, his product or the company he works for can be the basis for objections. However, these are usually not voiced out loud.

- **Service**
  For industries where the sale marks the beginning of a long-term customer relationship, such as agricultural machinery, heating systems, elevators, snow removal services, and webmaster services, objections are a common occurrence. Customers may raise objections because they will depend on the seller or service department for the long-term. Often, these objections only come to light after the initial purchase and experience with the product or service team.

- **Spare parts**
  The situation here is very similar to the topic of service, especially since spare parts availability can also

be seen as part of service. However, the availability of spare parts can also be an important argument for purchase or a reason for objection before a purchase is made.

- **Technical objections**
  These are objections that relate directly to the product or service. There are many variants. Such objections can be size, performance, duration, effectiveness, color, shape, and very much more. Each industry and even each offer has its own special variants.

That's about it, the most common purchase objections. Every now and then, an exotic variant comes up, but only as a real exception. What other basic objections do you hear regularly? Feel free to email them to me at service@romankmenta.com. I will be happy to include them in a new edition of this book.

As you may have noticed, objections can arise before, during, or after the purchase, in the form of complaints. In the course of this book, I will focus on how to deal with objections that you hear during a sales conversation, before your customer has even bought. However, you can also apply many techniques and strategies to complaint situations.

Your task: Preparation

Keep a record of the objections you frequently encounter in your sales practice. It shouldn't take you long - only five minutes or less. You'll be surprised if you have more than five to ten objections. This list will serve as the foundation for your next steps. By the end of this book, you'll not only have a list of the most common customer objections, but also strategies to effectively address each of them. This will greatly enhance your chances of closing a sale.

TYPES OF OBJECTIONS

Not all objections are the same. I am not talking about the content of the customer's statement. Rather, I am talking about the form, i.e. the way in which the objection is voiced, or the ulterior motives that play a role. The following distinctions are important because your approach should be aligned with them.

Strong and weak objections

Objections can be divided into strong and weak. In most cases, they can already be distinguished and classified very well according to the way they are raised.

A few examples of this:

Weak objections

- *"Would there be anything possible there on price?"*

- *"And a little earlier I can't have the product?"*

- *"I would like it a little better in a brighter red."*

- *"I would prefer it if you could deliver it."*

Weak objections could be formulated in this way or something similar. These are often packaged as questions or requests. The customer will tend to speak normally quietly, clear his throat, pause to speak, and have difficulty maintaining eye contact. He or she will appear less self-confident and perhaps even like a supplicant.

Of course, it may also be that in an individual case it is a strong objection that the customer raises very hesitantly and gently. Therefore, you must also perceive these objections in principle, but not necessarily take them seriously.

Strong objections

- *"The price is definitely way too high!"*

- *"I really need the product as early as Monday."*

- *"The red doesn't suit me at all. I need the lighter version."*

- *"I can't go get it. You have to deliver it."*

Strong objections are usually formulated in a more confident, direct and demanding manner - as a statement or command rather than a question. The customer's voice will also often be louder and stronger. He will maintain more eye contact. There is noticeable emotion in the way he speaks. He makes it clear: This is important to me.

From this, you already notice that it is an objection that you cannot or should not ignore, but have to take care of in one way or another.

Conditions

The most extreme form of a strong objection is a condition. Conditions must be fulfilled. They are particularly common in highly standardized purchasing processes, e.g. in the context of tenders. Normally, there is nothing to discuss or refute about conditions (as with a normal objection). Often, your interlocutor - even if he wanted to - cannot override these conditions.

We do not need to go further into conditions within the scope of this book. You can accept them or not. In the latter case, the customer will not buy from you, or you cannot make an offer at all. Your decision here lies primarily in the selection of the playing field on which you want to operate and whose rules you want to accept. Everything else would be a fight against windmills.

Apart from official conditions, as we find them in tenders or, more generally, in larger companies, there are also those that arise due to circumstances.

For example, a certain maximum width for a vehicle could be a condition, because otherwise, it cannot drive through the narrow gate at the entrance to the garage. Or the apartment must be barrier-free because the potential tenant is a wheelchair user. These kinds of conditions are not always set in stone, but - as objections - are usually extremely difficult to overcome.

Therefore, it is important to learn about these conditions very early in the sales process. If you cannot meet them, you will save a lot of effort and time.

Objections and Pretexts

Very exciting and extremely relevant for your handling of objections is the question of whether it is an objection at all, a true objection. Behind many an objection there is something quite different. In such a case, what you get to hear is a pretext. It is something that the customer puts forward to hide the real objection.

Why does he do that? That can have different reasons:

- **Your customer is embarrassed to voice the true objection.**
  This might be the case with price objections, for example. Instead of admitting that he can't afford or doesn't want something, your customer might instead criticize the fit or the color. Or a decision-maker may not be able to decide for himself at all because, for example, his wife or boss must agree. But to you, he has always acted as if he could make the decision on his own. Instead of saying what's the matter, he names another objection that buys him the time he needs to vote on the decision.

- **The customer's true objection would be immoral or even illegal.**
  This sounds a bit strange now, but there are industries in which illegal things definitely occur or are even the order of the day. Black money transactions can be found, for example, in the real estate industry, the construction industry or even in the trades. I don't want to point the finger at them. Rather, my aim is to make you aware that an apparent objection that has been voiced may also conceal a not entirely clean one that your customer is unable or unwilling to say.

- **Your customer wants to improve or not worsen his negotiating position.**
  In order to achieve a better price in a negotiation, your customer might introduce one or even several pretexts to put pressure on the price and improve his negotiating position. He might list the disadvantages of your product and even exaggerate so much that you yourself start to doubt your offer. These disadvantages can be real objections or just pretexts to get a higher discount.

- **The customer does not want to hurt you.**
  This can also be a reason to bring a pretext. Suppose you think that a photographer takes really bad photos. Would you tell him that or would you rather use a pretext like *"My boss had already decided on another photographer. Unfortunately, there's nothing more I can do"*?

There are certainly a few more reasons why your customer may not want to tell you their objection. The most important thing at this point is to be aware that what your customer says may not necessarily be the true objection. Be on your guard.

Outspoken and silent objections

Unspoken objections are either left unmentioned or replaced by a pretext, as previously discussed. Although expressed objections can be annoying or even frustrating, they are still crucial to improving and enhancing your closing rate. By addressing them openly and honestly, you can gain valuable insights and make positive changes to your sales approach.

Finding out silent objections

The question that many salespeople ask themselves is consequently: How can I distinguish objections from pretexts or bring an unspoken objection to light?

Not only in relation to objections, but also at many other points in the sales conversation, clever and psychologically effective questions are the means that will get you further. I'll show you a few of them in a moment, which are perfect for exactly this purpose. At the same time - since the topic is so fundamental - I would also like to refer you to the book "Well asked is half sold - Successful selling with psychological questioning techniques". There is hardly anything that is as important for you to master as a salesperson as the right questioning technique.

So how can you find out what the customer may have wanted to keep secret from you? There are two basic approaches to this. On the one hand, you can make statements that make it easier for the customer to come out with his true motives and thoughts, or you can ask specifically about it.

The Columbo Method

Do you know Inspector Columbo? Readers who are a little more experienced in life may still remember the crime series with the quirky but very clever investigator. But even the younger generations may have seen one of the reruns that are dug up again and again and shown on TV.

Columbo had a very special way of eliciting his suspects' secrets. He always pretended to be very harmless and innocuous, which tended to make the suspects careless. If he went out the door after talking to the potential perpetrator, or even just an important witness, he would often return a second later. He'd stick his head in the door again and ask another important question - along the lines of, *"I just thought of something else ..."*

Because he had already left, the suspects had relaxed and were more vulnerable to his new "attack" than they had been minutes before. As a result, he was able to learn things that had previously been hidden from him over and over again.

You can also use exactly this approach to find unspoken or even deliberately hidden objections. Ask again à la Columbo - after the sales talk is officially over and the customer may even have already decided against your offer:

- *"What else would interest me is, what was ultimately the real reason why you decided against our offer?"* In doing so, you are implying that he did not tell you. Now that everything is over anyway, the chances that the customer will tell you his hidden objections are much better than before. Especially if he did not mention them before in order not to worsen his negotiating position, this obstacle is no longer an obstacle.

But even if the decision to buy has already been made against your offer, you still have a (small) chance to get back into the conversation in the following way:

- *"Ah, I see, so that was it. If I had known that. In that case, we could make it so that we give you .... What do you think about that?"* - and you're back in the middle of the sales conversation.

Will it always work? No, of course not. But probably every reader has experienced a rejection that turned into an acceptance after all.

Inquiries for lost projects

This leads me to the strategy that I would definitely recommend to all those who work in consulting-intensive sales. They put a relatively large amount of effort and time into sales calls and - often written - offers. A rejection is particularly painful after such an effort. In that case, you should at least try to find out afterwards what hidden objections there were that prevented the purchase. Although this is usually of no use to you in a closed case, it does provide valuable information for your future business with this or other customers.

If you are dealing with a larger number of such projects or customers, you can also resort to a standardized and automated procedure. For example, send a link to a survey by e-mail to your non-customers, asking them what the reason or reasons were for not buying. You can provide several typical reasons to choose from, or (additionally) ask them outright.

This approach has the advantage that you can do this survey anonymously and should do it in case of a larger number. In this case, you are more concerned with the reasons than with the individual decision-makers behind them. Because of the anonymity, some customers may feel prompted to say more than they would in a conversation with you and to reveal their hidden objections.

As helpful as these approaches may be, they usually only help for future sales conversations. But what can you do to unmask pretexts and uncover hidden objections during the ongoing conversation? I have also brought you a few variants for this.

Social proof

If many people do something, then it can't be all wrong. This way of thinking is called "social proof" in psychology. To suggest to the customer that it is quite normal to have a certain objection, citing that many people or customers have this objection. This works especially well if you already have an idea of which objection still exists in secret.

How does it work? For example, like this:

- *"I hear from many of my customers over and over again that they think they can't afford the product. If you thought that too, it would be totally understandable at that price."*
  After that, keep silent and maintain eye contact. Your customer will feel prompted to answer by this "silent question" and will confirm or contradict what you have said.

- *"A common objection is that the product is too big for this use. How's that for you?"*

- *"Many customers criticize the long delivery time. You too?"*

This approach is already mixed with the following, which shows that separating these strategies is almost impossible and unnecessary. Mix them as it suits you.

Metacommunication

Metacommunication means stepping out of the topic of conversation itself and moving to a meta-level outside the conversation. From there, the conversation can now be viewed and talked about (instead of the content). Confusing? A few examples will make it much clearer right away.

Proceed roughly like this:

- *"Dear Ms. Sample Customer. We have been talking about the product for a while now and you keep bringing up critical points and questions. That's fine in itself, and of course you can criticize and ask whatever you want. However, I have the impression that there is more or something else behind it. What is it? Feel free to be quite frank."*
  Then you keep eye contact again and remain silent.

Alternatively, instead of asking the open-ended question *"What is it?"*, you can also work with a closed question. This always makes sense if you think you know what's behind it and you want to have this assumption confirmed. If you are right, your customer will often find it easier to answer a closed question than an open one:

- *"I have a feeling something is still bothering you. Do you perhaps have concerns about the price?"*

- *"It seems to me that there is something else that is holding you back from deciding on this product. Is it possible that you want to consult with someone else before you make the decision?"*

Keep in mind that, as mentioned above, the customer may be embarrassed to admit what the actual objection is, for example. Therefore, phrase it in such a way that your customer can admit it without losing face. Use soft phrases, use subjunctives, and reframe by turning negative statements into positive ones. Turn "get approval from the boss" into better "coordinate with the boss." I'll show you a little later what reframing is and how versatile and effective you can use this technique in objection handling.

Of course, metacommunication - regardless of the variant - takes a bit of courage. We are not used to talking about our communication with customers in this way.

Ask hypothetical questions

Another slightly more pressure-filled and conclusion-oriented method for getting to the bottom of hidden objections is to work with hypothetical conclusion questions. What do I mean by this?

The customer makes a critical statement, which could be an objection, but also a pretext. For example, he might say:

- Customer: *"The delivery time is too long for me."*

You do not yet know whether it is a real one or a pretext. To find out which of the two it is, proceed as follows:

41

- Salesperson: *"Is there anything else keeping you from buying the product?"*

Your customer now has two options: Either he says yes, in which case it was a genuine objection. Or he says no, in which case it was a pretext. Both are important for you to know.

If the customer answers yes, then ask:

- Salesperson: *"What else is there to clarify?"* - In a worst-case scenario, your customer will bring up additional defenses or excuses, which you can then review in the same way.

If the customer answers no, then proceed as follows:

- Seller: *"I understand, the delivery time is too long for you. May I ask by when we would have to deliver for it to be convenient for you?"*
  Customer: *"It would have to be by next week Tuesday."*
  Salesman: *"Does that mean if we can do it by next week Tuesday, you'll take it?"*

As you can see, things are already getting serious. If your customer still has objections at this point that he has not mentioned to you, he must mention them now at the latest. You leave him little room for other ways out. Either he tells you what the actual objections are, or he buys.

Use this very effective method with tact. Do not put too much pressure on the customer. To reduce the pressure, you can use vague, soft phrases.

Invite objections

The last variant for eliciting unspoken objections from your customer is no different in form from the previous ones. It is also about getting the customer to express his concerns by asking clever questions. The difference between this and the previous variants, however, lies in the intensity. Instead of just asking for possible objections "normally," you ask for them forcefully. What might that be?

- *"After there are always objections and concerns, what are yours?"*

- *"What else is stopping you from agreeing to our proposal?"*

- *"What we still need to conclude are the points that are still bothering you. What are those?"*

These requests to the customer to formulate his objections usually contain presuppositions. As the questioner, you assume that the customer has objections. The only question is: Which ones? Social proof", which we discussed earlier, is also included as an amplifier in one of the questions (in bold). This last variant for tracking down customer objections is therefore a mixed form.

With all these variations to distinguish pretexts from objections and to get on the trail of the real objections, you will not always be successful, but your results in sales conversations in the form of closes will always improve.

DO NOT RAISE OBJECTIONS AT ALL

W e've already talked about the fact that objections, when spoken, are not nearly as bad as their image or how they often feel spontaneously. They show interest on the part of the customer. Completely disinterested customers do not raise objections.

And yet, for many salespeople, it is of course, an ideal situation when no objections come from the customer and the customer simply buys because he is so convinced or even enthusiastic about the offer. That does happen. It depends very much on the product or the service offered. The more "perfect" this offer is for the customer, the more likely and more often this will be the case. It makes perfect sense to put a lot of energy into what you are offering. However, how to make your offer so compelling that your customer can only say yes is not the topic of this book. If you want to learn more about that, read the book "How to write offers that sell" (https://amzn.to/3HKXZT7). In it, you'll find 44 psychological strategies for successful proposal writing.

Rather, it's about working to sell your existing offering as well as possible. Even in this starting position, there is a strategy you can use to sell without hearing an objection from the customer. How to make it work? The basic idea behind it is simple: don't wait for your customer to bring an objection, bring it yourself. This is what we call objection anticipation.

Advantages, disadvantages and requirements

The approach of bringing up unspoken objections has its pros, but it also has a potential pitfall. The pitfall to watch out for is that if you raise an objection that wasn't on the customer's mind and that they wouldn't have thought of on their own, you could plant an undesirable thought in their head.

Your customer might take a liking to this objection and think to himself, *"Now that you mention it, there's something to it. Actually true."* You should always keep this potential danger in mind before working with this method.

This results in two important basic requirements that you should meet when using this strategy:

- Only mention objections that your customer already has in mind anyway and might voice sooner or later, or ones that your customer would still come up with if he or she thought further about the purchase decision.

- State only objections for which you can also show some kind of resolution. However, this may also mean that the objection does not resolve the negative itself, but can be more than outweighed by positive arguments.

If one of the two conditions cannot be met, then you should prepare for this objection as best you can, but keep it to yourself in case the customer brings it.

However, aside from the fact that you might be waking sleeping dogs, so to speak, by bringing objections to your own offer, there are some advantages for you as a salesperson to work with objection anticipation and state an objection or even several at appropriate times:

- **You have more control over it.**
  When you bring the objection to the table, you can choose the ideal time to do it. It can or should be a planned part of your sales conversation. From this point of view, the customer cannot surprise you with his objection (if you do not wait too long with it) and catch you on the wrong foot. He cannot catch you completely unprepared anyway, since you have prepared yourself well for all possible objections (or will do so in the course of the book).

- **You have already prepared your response to the objection.**
  While we're on the subject of preparation: If you bring up an objection yourself, you will still have prepared yourself much better to handle it in an appropriate manner than if the customer brings it up. This has to do, as mentioned, with the increased level of control you have with this strategy.

- **The customer feels understood by you.**
  When you say out loud what is already on your customer's mind, he feels understood by you. And making your customer feel understood is one of the most important things in a sales conversation. This is especially true when it comes to objections, as confrontation and counter-arguments are more expected and usually the norm in this phase.

- **Your customer is more focused.**

   As long as your customer has an urgent question or even a slowly emerging objection in his head, he is more or less preoccupied. He is distracted by it and not focused on what you have to tell him. In psychology, these "open loops" and unresolved issues that run through our minds are known as the Zeigarnik effect. According to this, we remember unfinished tasks much better than completed ones that we have mentally checked off. By naming and "handling" the objection, you help your customer mentally check off the issue.

- **It comes across as honest and builds trust.**

   A salesperson who says on his or her own initiative what can possibly be seen as bad or at least critical about his or her offer, or where possible disadvantages and pitfalls lurk, comes across as honest. Customers tend to expect the opposite from salespeople: to conceal disadvantages. With the strategy of anticipating objections, you, therefore, collect a lot of trust points on your relationship account with the customer. You can cash these in during the course of the conversation. Further statements you make will become more credible as a result of this approach.

All in all, I would say that the advantages of objection anticipation clearly outweigh the disadvantages. If you observe the two basic requirements mentioned and approach the matter with a bit of tact, you can certainly use this strategy successfully in your sales practice. The next question that now arises in this context is: How?

Objection anticipation - How to proceed

To anticipate and address potential objections, many sales-people use a technique known as FAQs (Frequently Asked Questions). This approach is a gentle way to prepare and respond to the most common objections that customers may have before they even bring them up. You can find FAQs on many websites, sales pages, and landing pages and they serve as a way to proactively address any potential objections. By having these answers ready, you can improve the chances of closing a sale and leaving a positive impression on your customers.

Of course, you can also incorporate these into sales pitches with the following phrases:

- *"I get asked more often if the delivery time can't be shortened."*

- *"A lot of our customers want to know if they can have the product in red."*

You can formulate this gentle way of anticipating an objection in this way or something similar, especially if you are not quite sure whether your customer is already thinking about it. The anticipation of the objection happens here BEFORE your customer mentions the objection himself, but AFTER you have made the statement - about the delivery time, the color, the price etc..

You can also take it up a notch and be a little more direct in your approach by "reading" the customer's mind - only instead of being in the form of a question, as in the Columbo method, it's in the form of a statement. If you want to give yourself a little leeway, however, you can raise your voice a bit at the end of the statement and put on your questioning expression, giving your statement the air of a question.

- *"You **may** think that the child safety lock on the stove is unnecessary for you, since you don't have children."*

- *"I'm **sure you're** thinking to yourself right now that this is way too much money for your area of operation."*

- *"You're **very likely** wondering right now if we can actually get this done in this short amount of time."*

You should proceed in this way rather when you are fairly certain that your customer is thinking of exactly that at this moment. You can moderate the directness of your statement by softening it with words like "probably" or "maybe" (or similar "softeners"), or by underlining it with "very" or "certainly".

You can also append a question at the end of your formulation, which might read, for example:

- *"Is that so?"*

- *"Am I right about that?"*

- *"Do you know it too?"*

If your statement is not true for the customer and the objection you formulated is not one for him, he will deny the question, and you can simply move on in your conversation. If he answers it in the affirmative, then you have the advantage of getting an endorsement from the customer (the yes to your assumption). This feels much better to both parties than an objection brought by the customer. Then you can handle or resolve the objection with your prepared response. The question at the end of the customer objection you have formulated also has the advantage that you retain control in the conversation because:

"Who asks, leads!"

But that's not the end of the line when it comes to objection anticipation. You can make your statement even stronger.

- *"Dear Mr. Test Customer, you're probably going to ask me to leave right now when I tell you that the prices are higher than you expected."*

- *"I have to tell you something now in terms of delivery times that you won't like at all. Shall I tell you anyway?"*

Unlike the previous versions, here you place the objection anticipation BEFORE the statement. You are anticipating an objection that the customer can't even have yet, because you haven't even mentioned the topic to which they might have an objection. I know that sounds a bit complicated (by the way, that's also an objection anticipation on my part). This approach also leaves room for a touch of theatrical exaggeration.

By the way, the last variant, in particular, can also be used very well in post-purchase situations when it comes to delivering bad news to the customer.

"Yes, but ..." - The good version

You may recall that earlier in the book, I quibbled with the "Yes, but ..." and condemned it as a mistake. I still stand by that ... except when you apply it as follows. Because then it is a very effective means of anticipating objections.

"But" weakens what is said before it and strengthens what follows it. That is, if you use it in the classic variant of a "Yes, but ...", it means that what the customer said is not true (although you say yes) and rather the opposite is true (what follows the but). So far, so bad.

But what if you use it as follows:

- *"This model costs real money, and not only when you buy it, but also every time you have to go to the gas station ... And believe me, you will soon know the gas station as well as you know your home. It's noisy, your neighbors will complain - every time you leave or come home. And you can't choose anything about it, you can only take it just as it is here. **But** the feeling when you roll down a curvy road on a beautiful summer day, then take a quick twist of the throttle on the straightaway and have to hold on tight to keep from being yanked off the seat ... That feeling is absolutely incomparable and worth every penny."*

That would be an - admittedly - somewhat more emotional and slightly exaggerated variant (perhaps put forward by a Harley-Davidson salesman). Of course, it can also be more factual.

- *"I have to tell you in all honesty, this model is a little more expensive and noisier and quite inflexible when it comes to trim levels, **but** the road holding and acceleration are like nothing else."*

Whether emotional or factual, this variant of "Yes, but ..." is a massive form of objection anticipation. You anticipate not just one possible objection, but a whole series of them, and you do so directly and openly. This sounds honest and sincere and makes what you say after the "but" seem even more positive and credible. If one is true, the customer assumes, then the other must also be true. In addition - and this is extremely important - the positive arguments come at the end and thus leave a positive overall impression, as you will read in the example in the next paragraph.

In a very short form, this technique was used in the 1980s by the anti-dandruff shampoo Crisan. The commercial said very confidently: *"Crisan is expensive as hell, but it works."* Compare that to the reverse: *"Crisan works, but it's expensive as hell."* If you weren't convinced of the significance of the sequence up to this point, you should be by now.

Labeling technique as an alternative to objection anticipation

As a small supplement to objection anticipation, I would like to give you another method that also leads to the customer not voicing his objection or, rather, not being able to voice it. Wait a minute; it's about to get a little clearer. This method is called the labeling technique and it works like this.

You would like your customer to behave in a certain way. For example, you want him to make a decision quickly, not haggle over discounts, or nag you about some technical and perhaps minor detail. To achieve this, you praise your customer for this behavior BEFORE he shows it. In doing so, you attach a label to him, so to speak (hence labeling technique), and attribute certain positive characteristics to him.

For example, if you want your customer to overlook the color of the product, which may not be perfect, and not bring any objection in this regard, you could use the labeling technique as follows:

- Salesman: *"Now we've known each other for a while. Do you know what I like about you, Mr. Mustermann?"*
  Customer: *"No!?"*
  Salesperson: *"You are someone who, based on your many years of experience, can see and judge the advantages of an offer very well, without constantly nagging about any potential disadvantages, as many others do."*

You have put your customer on a pedestal through this praise. And praise is difficult if not impossible, to defend against. Theoretically, he could knock himself off his pedestal:

- Customer: *"Well, you've got me all wrong. I'm also one of those yappers."*

In most cases, however, he will accept the praise with thanks. Objections to any less important things will then be very difficult for him to raise, because this would at least slightly tarnish the great picture you have drawn of him.

You can also use this method with other topics and thus specifically prevent objections from being raised. A few examples:

- *"You know, I love working with people who know what you want and then can make a decision quickly. You wouldn't believe how many indecisive people are out there."* (To forestall the "*I still have to think about it*" objection).

- *"Fortunately, Mr. Sample Customer, you are one of those people who have the patience for things that are really worth waiting for even a little longer. That's one of the things I appreciate about you."* (So that the customer can no longer bring his objection to a longer delivery time).

What objections do you hear more often and how can labeling technology possibly be used to address them?

At this point, an objection from your side would be perfectly understandable and appropriate: "Wait a minute, you said earlier that it is good if objections are voiced. But this method prevents exactly that." - True, you are absolutely right. The difference is that with the labeling technique, you're not merely covering up the objection and preventing the customer from voicing it, you're also persuading. By praising and putting yourself on the pedestal, the customer also begins to see himself a little bit in the light you would like to see him in.

In addition, the labeling technique is a strategy that is available to you. In which cases you use it and in which you prefer another one, that still remains your quite important decision.

Vaccinate - Anticipating the objections of others

But you can anticipate not only the customer's objections, but also the objections of others. What is meant by this?

Visualize a scenario where your customer makes a commitment and both parties reach an agreement, whether it's for a single point or the entire negotiation. So far, everything is going smoothly. But what if the person you're speaking with isn't the only one with a say or even the power to make a decision? What if his supervisor, partner, or even someone in his network who holds significant influence over him, objects to your customer's choice? It's also common for customers to back out of agreements.

For this reason, in some business areas, it makes a lot of sense to anticipate the objections of these co-decision makers or co-influencers.

- Salesman: *"Mr. Sample Buyer, I am very pleased that you have chosen this model. But, if I may be frank, I wonder what your wife will say when you get home with it."*

  With this wording, let the customer himself articulate his wife's potential objections.

  Customer: *"She'll ask me if I'm crazy to spend so much money on something like this."*

  Salesman: *"And what will you answer her?"*

As a salesperson, it's essential to anticipate objections that your customer may face. By preparing your customer ahead of time, you can strengthen their commitment and reduce the likelihood of them changing their mind. This approach is often referred to as "immunizing," as it protects the customer against objections from others. In this way, you can help ensure a smooth and successful sales process.

However, the salesperson can raise common objections himself instead of asking the customer for them:

- Salesman: *"I can already hear your boss saying that you could have gotten it cheaper somewhere else. How will you answer him?"*

- Salesman: *"Your husband will probably complain that it is taking twice as long as he would like. How will you argue that to him?"*

You can also inoculate your customer against their own future objections, protecting yourself from them confronting you in the future:

- Seller: *"You wouldn't be the first to call me the next day to cancel the purchase. I'm sure it's a great product, but it's still a lot of money."*
  Customer: *"Absolutely not. I've made up my mind and it's going to stay that way."*
  Salesperson: *"Are you sure?"* (If you want to add one more.)
  Customer: *"Absolutely sure!"*

Prepared in this way, this customer cannot become weak by any stretch of the imagination afterwards. And even if he does, he can no longer admit it to you.

A former customer and seminar participant, then a sales manager in the construction industry, developed his very own cheeky form of inoculation.

- Seller: *"I bet you that tomorrow morning you will withdraw from the purchase of the house."*
  Customer: *"Absolutely not."*
  Salesman: *"Then let's bet on a bottle of champagne - from the good one. If I don't hear anything like that from you tomorrow, then you've won and you get the bubbly. If you back out, then you owe me a bottle."*

Of course, this is not meant to be entirely serious, although betting debts are of course to be honored. At its core, it is the anticipation of a potential future objection, exaggerated and taken to extremes with a wink. Why not? There are certainly salespeople, customers, and situations where this approach also fits very well.

THE BASIC PROCEDURE

Before exploring the various techniques for handling customer objections, let's delve into the fundamental strategy behind it. This approach isn't suitable or effective in every scenario, but in many cases, it can serve as a foundation and be incorporated into other techniques. It's not just a strategy, but a mindset.

This strategy consists of five steps that will always be very similar to the same for all possible objections. This makes this method very easy and practical for you to use in your everyday sales life.

Objection handling in 5 steps

Step 1 - Listen, understand and show understanding

As mentioned earlier, one of the important skills in interpersonal communication is being able to listen. This is also true when your customer brings an objection. Let him finish, completely finish, and listen attentively. In communication, this is called "active listening" and includes the following elements:

- Maintain eye contact.

- Nod - not in agreement, but just to indicate that you understand and are listening.

- Say "Yes" or "Mmh" - as well just to show your understanding.

- Rephrase or repeat what was said, "The delivery time is too long for you, so say."

- Ask comprehension questions if necessary (we'll get to questioning the objection in a moment).

To effectively handle customer objections, it's crucial to start with a deep understanding of what the customer is saying. Miscommunications happen all too often, so taking the time to truly understand the customer's perspective is key. Showing the customer that you understand their objection goes a long way in building trust and rapport. This doesn't mean you have to agree with them, but showing empathy toward their point of view demonstrates that you're there to help find a solution. It's important to possess not just an understanding, but also a genuine connection and the ability to express that understanding to the customer.

This is an important first step and already a good portion of the rent.

Step 2 - Thank and appreciate

Thank the customer and show appreciation (I know, it's hard sometimes) for voicing their objection out loud. You remember, we've already talked about this too.

- *"I thank you for your openness on this point. I appreciate that very much, that we can talk openly about the things that are on your mind regarding the decision."*

Step 3 - Challenge the objection

Next comes one of the most important communication tools: questions. Objections are often very vague. For example, you may hear something like:

- *"It's been a long time coming."*

- *"I don't know if I like it."*

- *"The price is already high, though."*

All these are statements that lack one thing: concreteness. Therefore, you must specify the objection by means of so-called concretization questions:

- *"What exactly do you mean by 'a very long time,' or rather, how long is it likely to take?"*

- *"What exactly makes you doubt whether you'll like it?"*

- *"What exactly do you mean by 'high' in price and what is the maximum it should be?"*

Ask questions until it is clear to you and the customer what he means and you both have the same understanding of his statement. I experience time and again that customers often don't know exactly what they want to express with their objections. So by asking questions as a salesperson, you are also doing the customer a service. We will deal with the procedure of questioning the objection in much more detail a little later in the book.

Step 4 - Handle and resolve the objection

Only once you fully understand the objection, can you start working on a solution - if one is necessary or even possible. In the standard approach to handling objections, the solution would ideally be found here. However, as you will see in the methods of objection handling that follow, this fourth step can sometimes be skipped. But first and foremost, it's crucial to clearly comprehend the customer's objection.

However, I would also like to point out at this point that this short and inconspicuous step 4 can also conceal a long and difficult (negotiation) process.

Step 5 - Check the result

If you have managed to find a solution to the objection, then for a clean finish, it is recommended to check this solution e.g. as follows:

- *"So that means if we deliver it in the lighter green instead of, the darker green, that's absolutely fine with you?"*
  It is a question, but normally you will lower your voice at the end to make it seem like a statement. After all, you don't want to question the (hard-won) solution again; you just want to have it reaffirmed.

- *"Does this fit?"* - This option also lowers the voice.

- *"Does that conclude this item?"* - And also here.

With these five steps, you can solve a picture book canvas quite cleanly. It is helpful to know and have internalized this procedure, as it is the basis. However - as you probably know from your own practice - by no means are all objections picture book objections that can be resolved with the standard process. Therefore, I have brought a whole series of quite different variants and approaches for you shortly.

Instrument #1: Questions

The most important communication tool in the basics of objection handling is questions. Questions can be used so effectively in various communication scenarios that mastering questioning techniques is an absolute must for any professional communicator, including salespeople.

A SMALL REQUEST

Congratulations on exploring a variety of techniques to handle customer objections! I hope you have already put one or two of these strategies into practice and achieved great success. Remember, even if you only successfully implement one strategy from this book, you'll have already gained more than what you invested. That's the beauty of a well-written sales book- it pays for itself in no time!

As an author, it's crucial for me to understand how my readers are engaging with the book. I strive to constantly improve my writing based on reader feedback, making my books more informative and practical. If you have any additional insights or ideas from your own experiences, I'd love to hear from you! Simply send me an email at service@romankmenta.com.

Additionally, your support would mean the world to me if you left a review on Amazon or the platform where you purchased the book. If you feel confident in your assessment of the book after reading, feel free to leave a review now. If you'd like to finish reading the book before writing a review, that's perfectly fine too. Either way, thank you for your support!

Why am I writing this request now and not at the end of the book? Experience shows that something like this is easily overlooked at the very end. And now: Be curious about what is to follow.

METHODS OF OBJECTION HANDLING

In the previous section, we covered the fundamentals of handling customer objections. While this approach is often effective, it may not always be the right fit for every situation or objection.

Don't worry! In the following extensive section, you'll find a variety of tried-and-true strategies to handle objections in any situation. Some of these strategies may be vastly different, while others can be combined with the basic approach or even with other strategies.

By working with these strategies, you'll soon find the ones that are perfect for your industry, products, performance, and most importantly, your customers and the objections you typically face. With a range of approaches at your disposal, you'll be ready to handle any objection that comes your way.

It's now time to discover the best strategies for you to handle customer objections effectively. As you go through the book, identify which methods resonate with your sales approach and adapt them to suit your specific needs. Whether it's a combination of several strategies or a unique approach that works best for you, the key is to master these techniques through practice. With repetition, you'll be able to effortlessly apply the right strategy in any sales situation without having to consciously think about it. The ultimate goal is to reach a point where these strategies become second nature to you.

The following methods of dealing with objections are usually not individual methods but whole bundles of strategies, each of which is based on the same basic idea. For this book, I have summarized the possible approaches to objections in five such basic ideas:

- Basic idea 1: No resistance
- Basic idea 2: Create clarity
- Basic idea 3: Counterattack
- Basic idea 4: Role reversal
- Basic idea 5: Arguing and weighing up

Which strategy you choose or use in each case depends on the situation, the objection, and how it was brought.

Basic idea 1: No Resistance

As previously mentioned, the typical response to objections is resistance, often in the form of counterarguments. However, the approach of "no resistance" takes a different approach, inspired by Far Eastern philosophies, where the idea is that by offering no resistance, your customer's objections will have no impact.

Following this basic idea makes especially much sense when ...

- You rely on the fact that the customer buys, even if the objection remains unaddressed in the room,
  - because the advantages for the customer outweigh
  - or he has no other choices.

- The objection on the part of the customer is raised very weakly and with little emphasis.

- You cannot solve the objection even if you really want to.

- You can afford not to get the order.

What are the variants if you do not want to resist?

Ignore the objection

You can simply ignore the objection. This means that you hear it (which the customer is aware of), but do not react to it at all, but simply continue talking. Admittedly, this is an approach that can also have very negative consequences. You could be seen as arrogant. The customer - annoyed by your ignorance - might reinforce his objection or even bring more, along the lines of *"Well wait a minute, I'll show you. Now more than ever."*

Therefore, this approach is only suitable if you have a very strong position or if the objection was voiced very weakly and casually. But beware: You always run the risk of severely disturbing or damaging the relationship level with the customer.

Overhear the objection

Overhearing the objection is not the same as ignoring it. The significant difference is that, in this case, your customer has the impression that you have not noticed him. A small, but quite significant difference.

He now has two choices:

- He repeats his objection, this time probably a little louder and more clearly, so that you cannot overhear him again,

- or else he thinks to himself, "It wasn't that important anyway," foregoes the repetition and continues with the conversation.

In the first case, you must decide how to proceed. In the second case, you can tick off the objection (at least for the moment). If your customer already doesn't take his objection so seriously that he repeats it, why should it have any significance for you?

Change the theme

Instead of just ignoring or overhearing the objection, you can also - as an extension of these two variants, so to speak - change the subject. That means you attach the change of subject to ignoring or overhearing. In doing so, you have several options. What they all have in common is that the topic you change to is one that has a positive (or at least neutral) connotation in the customer's mind and to which he has no objections.

Compared to just ignoring or overhearing, this has the advantage that the communication continues and you make the customer think of something "nicer". You do this by means of a question you ask him about the new topic. What does this look like specifically? A few examples:

Change topic after ignoring

In dealing with objections, ignoring can be a powerful tool. To soften the blow of ignoring, try changing the subject immediately by briefly acknowledging the customer's objection and then smoothly transitioning with the word "And". Be careful, though, as the use of "Yes, but..." could potentially undermine the effectiveness of this technique. That's why the word "And" is so crucial in this scenario.

- Customer: *"I'm not sure I like the color."* Salesperson: *"I see. **And** what do you think of the finish?"*

  The "bad" version here would be, *"I see. **But** what do you think of the surface design?"* Judge for yourself how which variant affects you instead of the customer. The "and" expresses a certain appreciation of the customer's objection that the "but" completely lacks. It devalues the latter.

- Customer: *"The delivery time is already quite long."* Seller: *"I understand, the delivery time is a bit long for you. **Tell me, may I ask you something**? Customer: "Yes."*
  Salesman: *"Have you thought about where you will put the set in your living room? Where would it look particularly good?"*
  By including a brief permission to ask (in bold), you have elicited a yes from the customer, which makes a positive contribution to the course of the conversation.

As you can see, when combined with a change of topic, ignoring doesn't seem so ignorant anymore.

Topic change after overhearing

After overhearing, you cannot use understanding as a communicative stylistic device, since officially you have not heard the objection at all. You can still switch to another topic, with a clear cut, completely without transitions.

- Customer: *"How heavy did you say the device is? Five kilos? Pffft, that's not exactly light."*
  Salesman (in thought): *"Say, what's been bothering me all along, for the amount you're processing with it, wouldn't the slightly more powerful one be an option for you?"*

- Customer: *"Not exactly low, what the pool is supposed to cost."*
  Salesperson (in thought): *"Is there actually already a fixed date for the first pool party, where you want to inaugurate the pool with your friends?"*

It is important that your customer believes that you really overheard the objection. Therefore, this variant can only be used if the objection was actually overheard.

Agree with the customer

The next variant deals with the customer's objection more openly and offensively. The strategy is not to ignore or ignore, but to give clear and direct consent. This agreement can be based on two reasons or thoughts:

- What the customer criticizes is actually a disadvantage.

- What the customer criticizes looks like a disadvantage, but in reality, it is something that can also be seen as an advantage and that - at least you - are proud of.

If an objection concerns a real disadvantage, then you can either get rid of it or - if that is not possible or too costly - simply accept it. What else are you supposed to do with it. You pass the ball back to the customer. He must now decide whether to accept your offer - despite the disadvantage. With this approach, you as a salesperson gain strength and power in the conversation, regardless of how the customer ultimately decides. You don't apologize for the disadvantage, you don't try to talk it down, but you acknowledge it. Period.

- Customer: *"But the car is already quite wide."* Salesman: *"That's right. 202 centimeters, to be exact."*

- Customer: *"But the red is already very strong."* Salesman: *"That's right, I agree."*

One of my clients has made even less of an effort and answers "exactly" quite automatically in such cases. He is not put off by such an objection and simply continues to speak.

However, some objections are also very well suited for the second variant. Here, as mentioned, you make something good out of the point of criticism, an advantage. The customer should accept your offer not in spite of this point, but because of it. The objection thus becomes a buying argument. In detail, we will deal with the psychological method underlying this procedure, reframing.

This approach could be used for the following objections, for example:

- Something is very expensive. - A high price often means high quality and brings prestige to the buyer.

- Something exceeds the usual norm (size, weight, duration) and thereby possibly arouses a certain "pride of ownership" in the customer. This can even work for services that the customer does not "own" but only uses.

  o The biggest TV

  o The longest vacation trip

  o The highest office

  o The heaviest dining table

  o The strongest color

  o The most expensive consultant

And how could you express that linguistically? Go all out and exaggerate a little. Here are a few examples:

- Customer: *"But that's a lot of money for an apart-ment."*
  Seller: *"Absolutely right. In fact, it's the most expensive apartment I've ever sold, and - according to my research - the most expensive on the market in this area."*

- Customer: *"But that thing (TV) is already very big."*
  Salesman: *"Not only is it very big, it's currently by far the biggest we have in the store, and you'll be hard pressed to find a bigger one anywhere else."*

Of course, you could add a *"You wanted a really unique apartment"* or a *"Just right for your home theater"*. But at least in my opinion, you would take away the power and impact of your statement. It could be taken like a justification for the size. It's better to let your statement stand in space without further explanation and have an impact on the customer. Something so great speaks for itself and needs no further arguments.

Praise the customer

This variant builds on the previous one, agreement, and goes a small step further. Not only do you agree with your customer's objection, but (the bolded parts in the examples) you even praise them for getting it right.

- Customer: *"That's a lot of money for a cruise."*
  Salesperson: *"That's right, **you got that absolutely right**. It's the most luxurious cruise* (a helpful reinterpretation of the word "expensive") *you can get for your money."*

- Customer: *"But the dining table is much heavier than others. I can't move it on my own."*
  Salesman: *"Exactly. It's obvious that you've already dealt with furniture and its quality features."*

If you use this strategy, then you should definitely make sure that it is a sincere praise. Otherwise, the customer won't feel taken seriously or taken for a ride, and you'll be shot in the knee... into your own, mind you.

Basic idea 2: Create clarity

This basic idea deals with methods that help you create more clarity. This has already been covered as step 3 in the basic variant. However, as you will see, this idea holds many more possibilities than discussed in the basic variant.

Objections are very often, I would even say in the majority of cases, formulated relatively unclearly, as we have already established in the basic strategy for dealing with objections. The customer expresses a thought, sometimes just an emotion, without having thought about a clear formulation. Sometimes it is also a question that he asks and says out loud, perhaps even without expecting an answer from the salesperson:

- *"I don't know if I like the color."*

- *"That's a lot, though."*

- *"Quite heavy, that piece of equipment."*

- *"It's going to take that long?"*

In doing so, he gives a direction, but neither you as the salesperson nor he himself know what exactly he is trying to say. Therefore, this section deals with some variants of objection handling, which are all based on the basic idea of "creating clarity". These strategies in particular can also serve as the basis for other strategies that can be used or are necessary as soon as you have more clarity.

Ask questions

What probably won't surprise you is that questions are the most important tool for creating more clarity. Especially so-called concretization questions are in many cases the means of choice to find out and better understand what your customer really means with his objection. Concretization questions are always asked along the lines of "Who exactly? How exactly? What exactly?

- *"Who exactly makes the decision?"*

- *"How exactly do you want to proceed?"*

- *"What exactly do you mean by that?"*

- *"What exactly do you mean by that?"* (This and the previous question are universally applicable whenever an objection is unclear).

- *"(By) When exactly do you need the delivery?"*

- *"What exactly are you missing?"*

- *"What exactly is your budget?"*

If we take the above example objections, appropriate questions would be as follows:

- *"I don't know if I like the color."*

  o *"What colors do you like?"*

  o *"And how can you find out?"*

- *"That's a lot, though."*

  o *"What exactly do you mean by 'a lot'?"*

  o *"A lot or too much?"*

- ▪ *"By how much is too much?"* - If "too much" was the answer.

- *"Quite heavy, that piece of equipment."*
  - ○ *"How heavy can it be?"*
  - ○ *"Heavy or too heavy?"*

- *"It's going to take that long?"*
  - ○ *"What exactly do you mean by 'so long'?"*
  - ○ *"What's the maximum amount of time that you can take?"*

Ask for motives

If you ask in this way, you create more clarity, but basically still remain on the surface. It can be exciting if you dig deeper and research the actual motives for your customers' objections. There are hidden treasures that are worth searching for. It is the question of the customer's "why" that you can ask in various ways.

The direct why question

If you ask someone why they do or think something, there is a risk that the person you are asking will feel pressured. He may feel compelled to justify himself, and understandably he doesn't want to. You may also catch him cold with your "why" because he has never thought about the answer to it. For these reasons and others, your customer may react (slightly) angrily to your why question.

This does not mean that you cannot ask them. You just have to make sure that you ask them with flair. A simple and unadorned "Why?" without any helpful accessories would probably not meet this requirement.

- Customer: *"But your workshop is quite far away."* (Something that is an important factor in the agricultural machinery sector, for example).
  Seller: *"Why?"*
  Customer: *"Well, listen, 30 kilometers is a long distance for a tractor."*
  Salesman: *"Yes, but you don't drive them that often anyway."*
  Customer: *"Often enough. Too often, anyway."*
  Salesman: *"Well, the few more kilometers probably won't matter to you."*

A good example of how the why question doesn't work. Overdone? I don't think so. Such and similar examples can be seen every day in sales. Where this ends or where it doesn't end, we know. Presumably, the salesperson then reports to his boss that the repair shop is too far away for the customer. And that's something the supervisor can't blame his salesman for.

It could also go differently:

- Customer: *"But your workshop is quite far away."*
  Salesperson: *"What do you mean by 'quite a distance away'?"*
  Customer: *"Well, 30 kilometers is a long way, I think."*
  Salesperson: *"And what wouldn't be far for you?"*
  Customer: *"Anything up to 20 kilometers, I would say, is okay."*

Salesman: *"The closer the better, I understand that.* **But may I ask why this seems so particularly important to you***?"*

Customer: *"With my old tractor, I had to go to the shop every two weeks, so the distance added up nicely."*

Salesman: *"I can understand that. That means that if you only have to take our tractor to the workshop twice a year, then the distance doesn't matter?"*

Customer: *"No, not then."*

Salesman: *"That means what you're really concerned about is not so much the distance to the workshop, but having a reliable vehicle that drives instead of sitting in the workshop."*

Customer: *"Yes, you could certainly look at it that way."*

In this case, has the customer already bought? No, anything can still happen and prevent the purchase. But the chances are upright. What the seller has added in support in the second case is a permission to ask:

- *"... May I ask ..."*

This approach takes some of the edge off the why. If you want your why to be welcomed even more warmly by your customer, then also give them a reason (in bold) along the way:

- *"The closer the better, that's clear to me in principle. However, I have the impression that this point is particularly important to you.* **So that I can really**

> **understand your motives here**, *may I ask you why that is?"*

It is unlikely that any customer will refuse to answer a question formulated with such understanding and prudence, if they know it at all. And if that should still be the case, then your problem with this customer lies somewhere else entirely - probably in the relationship level.

Ask for goals

Even when phrased carefully, the question of why tends to be directed at the status quo or the past. You can take your search for clarity in a completely different direction by making a small change. What if, instead of looking for an explanation for the customer's behavior or opinion, you wanted to find out where they are going or what their goals are?

Let's stay with our example of agricultural machinery once again:

- Customer: *"But your workshop is quite far away."*
  Salesperson: *"What do you mean by 'quite a distance away'?"*
  Customer: *"Well, 30 kilometers is a long way, I think."*
  Salesperson: *"And what wouldn't be far for you?"*
  Customer: *"Anything up to 20 kilometers, I would say, is okay."*
  Salesman: *"The closer the better, I realize that. Tell me, may I ask you a completely different question that has nothing to do with the distance of the workshop?"*
  Customer*: "Ask."*

Salesperson: "So what are your plans for your farming operation?"

Customer: "I'm 60 now, and I want to slowly hand over the business completely to my junior."

Seller: "And should everything stay the same there?"

Customer: "No, he has plans. He always says that we have to grow to stay competitive. He wants to lease a lot of land to do that. There's a piece of land right around here."

Salesman: "This means that our workshop would be in your operating area in the future?"

In dealing with objections, especially one about distance, questioning techniques can come in handy. Ask your customer about their goals, this may help to weaken the objection, or even resolve it. However, there may be instances where your customer has no clear goals, or you are unable to find anything useful. Nevertheless, it is worth exploring your customer's goals as it can still bring positive results.

If you do this early on (as part of the needs assessment) rather than after the objection has been voiced, this can give you good material for objection handling:

- *Salesman: "You mentioned at the beginning that your business is being expanded and that you are thinking about leasing space here around the corner from us. Then we would be perfectly placed, so to speak."* Customer: "Yes, that would be the case."

There is no longer any need for an objection, because there is no objection. Quite the opposite. The potential objection has become an argument in favor of buying from this supplier.

Therefore, deal with the customer's goals. If what you find is not what you need to deal with the objection, this information will certainly be very helpful elsewhere. And too much knowledge about the customer has never hurt any salesperson.

Repeat

But a question to clarify an objection does not have to be voiced at all. It is often enough to simply repeat the customer's objection, just as is done in active listening.

- Customer: *"That's pretty elaborate, though."*
  Salesperson: *"I see, you think that's pretty elaborate."*

Then maintain eye contact and wait for the customer to say something. Normally, he will begin to explain what he means by this. Often, however, he will not only provide a neutral explanation for it, but rather some kind of justification (in bold) for his objection or for having voiced it in the first place.

- Customer: *"Yes, I **just** wanted to say that I don't have any experience with this product and that I think it could be more time-consuming. But you probably get the hang of it after a few times and then it's easier."*

In this example, the customer even weakens his objection himself, partially retreats and even brings arguments that invalidate his objection. Seen in this light, this approach also fits into the "Counterattack" section, which we will discuss in detail later.

The competitive comparison

A common concern among customers is that a competitor's offer may be better or cheaper. This is a prevalent issue across numerous industries, where customers are faced with a plethora of options and want to make an informed decision. As a result, it's not surprising that comparison shopping is a common occurrence.

When facing objections, it's common for customers to compare your offering to that of your competitors. This can be seen in almost every industry, where customers are presented with multiple options to choose from. To make the best decision for themselves, they compare different factors such as size, weight, horsepower, duration, and more. However, sometimes these comparisons are based on individual tastes and preferences, as a customer might simply say "I like your competitor's model better." In these cases, it's important to delve deeper and create clarity around the comparison criteria.

Even with criteria such as prices, it is sometimes not at all clear what the customer means when he says that the competitor's offer is cheaper (more on this shortly). In the case of complex products or services, which may also be financed with loans or leasing, it is often not even clear what the price is.

If your customer is using other offers for comparisons, you usually need to take action. You need to prevent apples from being compared with pears - or in some cases with sauerkraut.

If you are now trying to find out more about the customer's comparison, it can be useful to focus first on the criteria or his approach on the basis of which he compares. Therefore, ask e.g.:

- *"What are the criteria you use to compare our offer?"*

- *"When you compare, how do you go about it exactly?"*

- *"To be able to compare two such offers, you need good expertise and a certain procedure. I find that sometimes it's not easy with such complex offers. Therefore - so that I understand this better - my question: how exactly do you do that?"*
  By doing so, you bring in a little praise for the customer by implying that they have know-how and a good strategy for comparing.

It is entirely possible that your customer has no clear criteria for his comparison and relies solely on his gut instinct. In this case, you can assist him in determining his comparison criteria by asking the following questions.

- *"Possible criteria to compare such offers would be A, B, C .... which one do you use for your comparison?"*
  (By suggesting comparison criteria, you make it easier for the customer to find his).

- *"What do you think would be good criteria to make such a comparison?"*

When searching and selecting the criteria, you naturally influence the result. On the one hand, you should ensure that all particularly relevant criteria are used. On the other hand, the majority of the criteria should be ones in which you perform better than the offer being compared. If these are still too few, then bring criteria into play where this is the case. Even if these may not be as relevant from an objective point of view, you will still shift the comparison in your favor.

Once you have more clarity on the comparison criteria and strategy (if there is one), you can turn to the competitor and ask about:

- *"When you say competitor, who do you mean?"* - Sometimes the name of the competitor already tells you whether it's another type of apple, a pear, or sauerkraut.

- *"Who exactly are you comparing us to?"*

- *"What exactly did the competitor offer you?"*

- *"Could you show me the quote so we can compare together?"*

- *"What do you say we put the two offers side by side and compare them point by point? Then you can see even more clearly where the advantages lie for you in our offer."*

Of course, your customer will not always willingly give you information or even show you the competitor's offer. Often, he fears that this might weaken his negotiating position if he reveals his secrets. Sometimes he is not allowed to do so. Equally, however, there are cases where customers actively offer such a comparison on their own initiative in order to challenge you to make a better offer.

With some of the procedures or questions listed above, you must also be careful not to leave the impression that the customer himself cannot compare correctly.

If you now have the required information (list of criteria or offers and prices of the competitor), you can either - together with the customer - compare the two offers point by point (if possible) or create a separate list with the criteria relevant for the customer (and yourself). You can then rate them according to a specific evaluation scheme (e.g. 1 - 5 points). Even if your offer is clearly better than the competitor's, you should make sure that there is at least one category in which you do not do badly, but the competitor does slightly better. This will make the result of the comparison more credible and convincing.

You can make this comparison together with your customer on your notepad. Especially if there are more than three criteria that are used, I would recommend doing this in writing. Otherwise, there is a great risk that your customer will no longer have an overview ... and neither will you.

	Product A	Product B
Availability	+	~
Price	~	+
Durability	+	~
Weight	+	−
Design	+	+
	⊕	

The aim of the whole search for criteria and the comparison is to collect more plus points than the comparison offer. Especially if you have made the comparison cleanly directly with markings on the written offer or by hand sketch, this has a convincing effect. The customer can then make his own decision based on this clear comparison - hopefully in your favor.

Costs or prices?

Especially when objections are about prices, clarity is very important. What does the customer mean when he says "too expensive". You don't know at that moment, not yet. Even what the price is, is often not that clear with complex products and services (and often a combination of both in one offer). There are one-time payments and ongoing costs, or costs that are only charged in certain cases.

When it comes to the price of a bottle of mineral water, it's all quite simple. If you sell an industrial plant or parts of it, put it into operation and then also operate it for the customer, that's a completely different matter. But it doesn't have to be that extreme. Even a relatively simple product like a car allows for leeway, as you'll see in a moment.

Now there are many different approaches to dealing with price objections. So many, in fact, that I have written my own book on the subject: "Price objection handling made easy - 118 proven sales tactics". If you want or need to deal with price objections in a particularly intensive way (because you are often confronted with them), then you will certainly find what you are looking for in this book. You will find many of the strategies in this book, but they are always related to price objections. A special book, so to speak.

www.romankmenta.com/shop

One approach that is useful and applicable specifically to price objections is to be clear about whether the customer is talking about the cost or the price of a product or service. Therefore, I would like to single this out as an example of the many variants of dealing with price objections.

A classic example from car sales (when it comes to comparing prices on different but "equivalent" models):

- Customer: *"But this is already expensive?"*
  Salesman: *"May I ask: do you mean the price or the cost?"*
  Customer: *"I don't understand what you mean?"*

> Seller: *"Sorry if I was unclear. By price, I mean what you pay when you buy. The cost is the amount you'll pay when you add up everything that's involved in running it and then break it down to a per-mile amount."*

The salesman can now provide clarity in terms of money and use cost comparisons per kilometer for this purpose. But in doing so, he has not only gained more clarity, he may also have changed the criteria according to which the customer makes his decision.

This strategy has a long tradition in the sale of automobiles. Trade journals like to compare the costs per kilometer of different vehicles. It is not uncommon to find that a vehicle with a higher price performs better in terms of cost than competitor models.

But this kind of objection handling is applicable not only to vehicles, but to very many other products and even services. Sometimes you just need to modify the approach a little for this. Of course, kilometers are not always the unit of measurement by which you can compare. Here are a few examples:

- Shoes, handbags, or higher quality clothing quite generally per one wear,

- Vacation per day, taking into account arrival and departure costs and any included or non-included services as well,

- Elevators, chairlifts, or cable cars per passenger transported, per hour of operation, or per trip,

- Trainings and seminars per hour or per participant (per hour).

What are units of measurement that make sense for what you offer as a benchmark and make your offer score better in the comparison?

Of course, you can make these number comparisons not only for costs, but also for revenues or savings. For some offers, it's the same coin - just looked at from two sides. If you offer heat-insulating facades for houses, for example, you can of course compare the costs on the one hand, but also the savings on the other. Are there also savings in your area that you could cite?

Basic idea 3: Counterattack

Objections from customers are often perceived as an attack by the seller, but this isn't always the case. It can be a simple question that can be easily addressed with a quick answer, or it can be a more challenging argument. In either case, our natural instinct is to either fight back or flee.

In sales, fleeing is not an option, so we often resort to defending ourselves. However, as we've learned, defending our offer can have negative consequences. So, what alternative do salespeople have to handle objections effectively?

Following the basic idea of this section, we can - instead of merely defending - go a bit further and start a counterattack. In doing so, we take the customer's objection as something that helps us move a (nice) bit in the direction of our conversational goals. The counterattack (I apologize for this militant term, of course, a customer conversation should have nothing of a fight. I just haven't thought of anything more appropriate to date) can have the following positive effects in the process:

- It strengthens the seller's back and consolidates his position.

- It increases the customer's desire to accept the offer.

- It surprises the customer, unsettles him and makes him rethink his position.

- It brings the salesperson directly to the close in some cases.

- It entails concessions from the customer for the seller.

- It turns the customer into an ally.

All in all - you could say - it feels very good for you as a salesperson if you don't just defend yourself when you get an objection, but take action. After all, it is your job as a salesperson to set the direction and say where things are going ... And you can only do that if you have the rudder in your hand.

As for the specific strategies and approaches that follow from this basic idea, there are several, some quite different, that you can use individually or in combination.

Rejection and withdrawal

Even if this may seem strange at first glance: It can be a form of counterattack if you use an objection as an opportunity to move in the opposite direction. Instead of moving in the direction of closing the sale, you pull back.

This strategy makes sense, especially if you ...

- know (or at least are quite sure) that the customer is very interested in your offer.

- have no way to get the objection out of the way.

- are not dependent on sales.

- want to sell the last product of its kind that you have in stock and know that in any case you can quickly sell it elsewhere.

- have a great deal of conversational power in relation to the customer.

- Want to make your offer even more attractive and increase customer desirability.

- want to build more power in the conversation.

What might that look like or be in concrete terms?

- Customer: *"But the pool is already very big."*

Following this strategy, the salesperson could now respond with the following statements (a few different variations):

- *"Too bad, I thought we were going to do business."*

- *"I guess your pool won't be happening then."*

- *"Then I'm sorry, I can't help you there."*

With formulations like these, you are throwing out the baby with the bathwater. You conclude from the customer's objection that he does not want to buy - because of his objection. In most cases, of course, you are exaggerating. After all, a single objection to possibly only one decision criterion does not mean that your customer will not buy because of it. Of course, you know that, too, which is why you rely on this approach to ensure that your customer sees it the same way.

It's a bit like putting something in someone's hand, they grab it and look at it with interest, and then you take it away. Physically, this often has the effect that your counterpart wants to grab it and take it back. After all, it was already (almost) his. If you have doubts about the strategy, give something to a small child and then take it away again. The reaction is predictable. We may grow up and become adults, but certain behaviors are so deeply ingrained that they don't fundamentally change.

If your customer is still interested in your offer despite his objection, then he will start to rebut his objection and row in the opposite direction. Perhaps he himself voices what I have just described:

- Customer: *"Well, just because the pool is bigger than I thought doesn't mean I don't like it."*

And what if the customer doesn't back down? Of course, this strategy can also backfire, and that's if you've played the poker a little too high. But if you don't have a problem with the customer not reacting as expected for the reasons mentioned above, then at least you know where you stand.

The body language as an amplifier

To reinforce the effect of your retreat and to appear even more credible, you should emphasize the whole thing with body language. In concrete terms, you can ...

- Slamming your records,

- put away the offer,

- put the product away,

- lean back (because before that you will probably both be leaning forward),

- put away the pen (if you have one in your hand).

If you retreat only verbally, but do not signal in body language that you are serious, you are not very credible. When the message expressed in content differs from the message expressed in body language, we tend to give more credence to what the body is saying.

Train by train

Imagine receiving a birthday gift from a loose acquaintance you meet maybe once every two years. For the first time. You had never given each other anything before. Nothing big. A little something, a bottle of wine, a box of chocolates, or even just a nice card. What are you thinking now?

If you tick like most others, there are two things that run through your mind, *"What does he want from me?"* and *"Crap, what am I going to get him?"* When we receive a gift unexpectedly from almost strangers, we automatically (and often rightly) assume an intention behind it. We know that - once we accept it - we are in the other person's debt. The second question then clearly expresses that we are obliged - whether we want to or not - to reciprocate with a gift of roughly equal value. Rightly, you are now asking, *"And what does that have to do with dealing with objections, please?"*

As the example shows, we are used to giving something when we get something. In behavioral psychology, this behavior pattern is called reciprocity. This in turn means that it may well be appropriate to respond to customer demands, as is more often the case with objections, with a counter-demand. The customer will understand this (unconsciously and quite automatically) because it is a learned pattern, a behavior that has already been practiced very frequently.

One example:

- Customer: *"The delivery time is too long for me. I need it by the end of next week."*
  Seller: *"I can see if I can do something for you. It will not be easy. If I can do it, then there will be an additional cost for you in the amount of 75 euros and I need the order from you immediately."*

- Customer: *"The green does not match our corporate identity."*
  Salesperson: *"I could try to get the factory to produce a special color for you. What kind of green do you want?"* (Note, instead of enumerating what types of greens are possible, the salesperson is asking a direct closing question here).
  Customer presents a color sample: *"This one."*

Seller: *"Then I'll be happy to request this for you. The delivery time for this is two weeks longer at an additional cost of 200 euros. Shall I order it?"* (That's how quickly you can go from an objection to a conclusion).

These are just a few simple, everyday examples. Make sure that whatever you make possible for the customer is a little difficult, tedious, and uncertain. After all, you want something in exchange for this extra effort from the customer, whether it's a surcharge, an immediate order, or even a little more patience. Of course, this approach makes sense only if there is a solution to the customer's objection.

However, depending on the situation, you can also push the move-by-move strategy even further and push it harder, i.e. become more demanding. This can be particularly appropriate if the customer has a greater demand that is associated with an objection.

- Customer: *"The part is definitely too long."*
  Salesperson: *"What do you mean by 'too long'?"*
  Customer: *"Well, it should be 90 centimeters long at the most."*
  Salesman: *"By default, we offer it in 95, 100 and 105 centimeters. Would you be willing to take five then, because then I can try if we can get a special size from our supplier?"*
  Customer: *"I only need one, what am I going to do with five?"*
  Salesman: *"How long have you been using one?"*
  Customer: *"I don't know, this is my first one. I haven't used these before. Do you know how long it will last?"*

Seller: *"Three to six months usually. You don't have to worry about it for the next two years."*
Customer: *"And how much does the special production cost."* (The word "special production" automatically makes the customer accept that there is a surcharge associated with it).

There is another variant in which you do not even make the counterclaim yourself, but pass the ball back to the customer. You can use this very well for price objections, for example:

- Customer: *"I still need a concession from you on the price."*
  Salesperson: *"And how would you accommodate me for that?"*
  Customer*: "Why, I would buy!?"*
  Seller: *"YES already, at the offered price. But if I would still meet you with the price, then it is only fair if I also get something from you in return."*
  Customer: *"Mmmh. I could imagine buying the next product I need in two to three months from you then?"*

Of course, as a salesperson, you can also (still) bring suggestions as to what the customer could do for you. However, if you pass this ball back to the customer, he may come up with ideas that you would not have had at all. And besides: He who asks, leads.

Reverse logic

When the customer brings an objection, we usually automatically interpret it as something "negative." But what if we don't do that? What if we assume - just hypothetically -

that this objection speaks FOR our offer instead of AGAINST it? This won't work for all objections, but it brings both the salesperson and customer to interesting new ways of looking at some objections.

A few simple examples:

- Customer: *"But the red is already very strong."* Salesperson: *"True, it reduces the risk of accidents because you are seen much more quickly."*

- Customer: *"But the delivery time is already very long."*
  Salesman: *"That's right. That means you can go on vacation beforehand and relax and make the preparations for the installation afterwards."*
  Important: Do not insert a "but for this ..." here. This would be a justification.

As you may have noticed, this variant of dealing with objections also involves agreement in the vast majority of cases (see Basic Idea 1: No Resistance).

The basis for this reverse logic is the so-called "reframing". It could also simply be called "giving a different meaning" or "reinterpreting". This is a method that is widely used in NLP (Neurolinguistic Programming). On closer inspection, it is something we frequently use in everyday language, usually without noticing it.

There are several variations in the use of reframing. The following are particularly helpful in dealing with objections:

- Reinterpreting individual words or entire statements,

- Replacing individual words or rephrasing entire statements.

Reinterpret

When reinterpreting words or statements, you give a different meaning to what the customer says (as in the examples above).

- Customer: *"This price is beyond my budget."*
  Seller: *"All the more reason to finance the purchase instead of paying cash."*

- Customer: *"But the device is quite heavy."*
  Seller: *"That's right. This also dramatically increases its stability."*

- Customer: *"But the production time is already long."*
  Seller: *"Exactly. That means we have enough time to do the important things with the care we need."*

Instead of viewing the customer's objection as a hindrance to making a sale, try seeing it as an opportunity to enhance the financing. Reframing objections in this way may not always work, but with the right level of creativity and preparation, it can be a powerful tool in your sales arsenal.

However, relying solely on improvisation skills may not be the most practical approach. It's always better to be prepared for potential objections by researching and anticipating what your customers may raise. Nevertheless, there may still be cases where a suitable reframing cannot be found. But don't worry! This book offers many other methods that can help you overcome objections and close more sales.

Replace

The second type of reframing I would like to talk about is the substitution of words or phrases. The boundary to reinterpretation is fluid here, but it doesn't matter whether what you do is one or the other ... The main thing is that it gets you somewhere.

A few examples of terms you can replace with others to change the meaning of the statement:

- Stressful <> much to do
- Problem <> Task (Challenge)
- Expensive <> valuable
- Boring <> relaxing
- Too big <> powerful (still leaves room for maneuver)
- Tight <> figure hugging
- Bad <> not yet perfect
- Ugly <> eye-catching

It will often be the case that you replace a customer's negatively associated word with a more positive one in order to at least mitigate the objection.

- Customer: *"That's a real problem with the hourly output."*

Salesperson: *"Yes, we still have a problem to solve.*
Customer: *"Definitely."*

This way, you do not contradict the customer, but even get his agreement ("definitely"). Thus, the new meaning is anchored and "having a task to solve" is nothing fundamentally bad. Contradiction could create resistance from the customer, as in this negative example:

- Customer*: "The hourly thing is really a problem."*
  Seller: *"Well, I wouldn't call it a problem."*
  Customer: *"But I do."*

When you use substitution, be sure that the meaning of the new term is not too far from the term that the customer used. The distance should be only enough for the customer to accept it.

In the gentlest version, you just repeat the customer's statement as a sign that you are really listening well (active listening), but with slightly changed words.

- Customer: *"So the content for the seminar is not what I want for my salespeople."*
  Salesperson: *"I see, the contents are **not yet optimal.**"*
  Customer: *"Yes, we need to change that a bit."*

"Not yet optimal" is always a little better than "... not what I want" and was apparently accepted by the customer in this example.

Negative reframing

It should also be mentioned that you can also use reframing in the other direction, by replacing a positively associated term with a more negative one, or giving it a negative meaning. This probably sounds a bit strange and you may wonder why you should do this. There may well be situations in the sales conversation or objection handling where this makes sense.

- Customer: *"The Model X from your competitor is still 30 centimeters longer and offers correspondingly more space inside."*
  Salesperson: *"That means it's a challenge to find a suitable parking space in often tight parking lots."*
  (Reframing by reinterpreting)

- Customer: *"At the moment, I'm quite stress-free there."*
  Salesman: *"I see, that means you run the risk of getting bored."*

As you can see from these two examples, reinterpretation can hardly be separated from substitution. Admittedly, you will be able to use positive reframing more often than negative reframing, but knowing this variant as well won't hurt at all.

Degree Orientation

Objections are sometimes a real invitation to close the sale. The path from the (handled) objection to the customer's final yes is often a very short one. It's a bit like judo: you can convert the energy of the objection into closing energy.

First, as mentioned earlier, the fact that your customer raises an objection also means that he is basically (still) interested. If all interest had already been extinguished, he probably wouldn't bother or wouldn't talk to you at all. Of course, it is not possible to generalize how this behaves in the particular situation. It always depends on the content of the objection and the way it is raised. But if your customer is interested, a deal is possible.

Secondly, in many cases it is not at all illogical to assume that - if you can solve the customer's problem or question and thus eliminate the objection - the customer will buy. This is especially conceivable if it is the only objection he still has.

In order to turn the energy of the objection into closing energy and use it directly to close the sale, it is important to adopt this mindset as yours.

The last objection

This way of thinking is the basis for a method of handling objections that is very effective and can be used excellently for various types of objections. It is called "The Last Objection" and when you get to know it right away, you will find that the name says it all.

Basically, after your customer has stated an objection, there are two more points to clarify in order to reach a conclusion:

- Is it the only objection that the customer still has and

- does the customer buy when you solve the objection?

So how do you go about the "last objection" now?

You already know the first steps of the method from the basic variant of objection handling:

Step 1 - Listen, understand and show understanding

Step 2 - Thank and appreciate

From now on, the conversation proceeds somewhat differently. Before you question the objection (as in the basic variant), first narrow it down further:

Step 3 - Narrow down the objection

In this step, you need to find out whether the present objection is the last and therefore the only one (hence the name of the method) or whether there are others. And you do that with the following simple but very effective question:

- *"Is there anything else that would prevent you from choosing our offer?"* (A closing question in which there is the pre-assumption that a purchase by the customer is quite conceivable).

The customer now has two options: "Yes" or "No". If he answers yes, it means that you do not yet have to address the objection raised. Obviously, there are others that need to be known and explored. The logical inquiry in this case is:

- *"And what is that?"* or in a little more detail, *"And what points do we need to clarify before you can decide on that?"*

This will give you a collection of objections (hopefully not too many) to work through one by one. Normally, however, there will usually be only one further objection. Your customer has probably had this in mind for some time. Because you put him under a little pressure with the closing question, he now has to name it. You see, this way of asking creates clarity. Your customer has to show his colors and you know where you stand. You also signal to your interlocutor that "things are getting serious" and that the decision to buy is imminent. A gentle but clear nudge.

If your customer answers no - in the sense of *"No, there's nothing else"* - you are close to closing the deal. Only this one objection stands in the way of the purchase. If you get around it, overcome it, sufficiently mitigate or resolve it, you have reached the goal of the conversation - closing the sale. In this case, you can move on to the next step.

Step 4 - Challenge objection

At this stage of your conversation, the kind of questions we discussed in the "Creating Clarity" chapter are helpful.

- *"What exactly do you mean by 'too expensive'?"*

- *"When you say it takes you too long, what does that mean exactly?"*

- *"What color would it have to be for you to decide on the product?"*

As the examples show, the approach can be applied to a wide variety of objections and can be very helpful especially with price objections

What the customer gives you as an answer can be a task that is solvable for you or one that is not so solvable. If the customer needs delivery by Monday, but you can't deliver until Wednesday at the earliest (even if you try hard), then you can stop this approach here and communicate very clearly that this is not possible.

However, "the last objection" is interesting for all those cases in which you can solve the objection - easily or even by exerting all available forces. If that is the case, then you can move on to the next step.

Step 5 - Obtain commitment

If we should now have a - perhaps even simple - solution to the objection, we tend to reveal it quite automatically and immediately. We are relieved that we can solve it so quickly and easily.

- Customer: *"It should be in this red here."*
  Salesman: *"Yes, we can do that as a custom job."*

That may be a good feeling, but critically asked: Do you, as a salesperson in this example, now already have a commitment from your customer? - No, you don't. Because it could go on like this:

- Customer: *"Good to know. I'll think about it then."*
  (Exit customer)

Too bad, now that you could solve the objection so quickly. Will the customer come back? Maybe. But the probability has just dropped a little. Anything could come up.

It is, therefore, better not to let the customer off the hook so easily at this point:

- Customer: *"It should be in this red here."*
  Salesman: *"Mmmh, if we can do it - and I'm not quite sure yet - do you want it in red?"*
  Customer: *"Yes."*

Where is the difference from the previous variant? The salesperson has asked a hypothetical closing question. That means he got the customer's commitment BEFORE even trying to resolve the objection. And that's a world of difference from solving the objection and then hoping for the commitment.

After all, it might take some effort on your part to resolve the objection and - as in the example - get production to produce a variant with a special color. Why bother if the customer doesn't even know if he wants the product in the first place.

As a keen reader, you may have already noticed a crucial detail in the salesperson's approach. They presented the solution to the objection as if it were a challenge. This is an extremely effective strategy from a sales psychology perspective, and one that you should definitely consider utilizing - regardless of whether the solution is actually difficult or quite simple. By doing so, you add an air of exclusivity to the solution, making it more desirable. This same principle can be seen in the "Rejection and Withdrawal" section, where we explore the power of creating scarcity. By making the solution to the objection seem rare, you increase the interest and desire for the product.

Yes, I confess, this is causing you to cheat just a tiny bit. Maybe your conscience can live with it if you tell him it's for a good cause - closing the sale - which is ultimately what you AND the customer want. He is not talking to you just for fun either.

But what if the customer answers no? Well, even then you are helped. You know where you stand and have a little more clarity. Logically, the following question would follow a no from the customer:

- *"I see. May I know what the reason is that you are not yet convinced?"*

In itself, a no answer is not logical. Your customer had already answered no in step 3 to the question *"Is there anything else that prevents you from choosing the offer?".* Consequently, he would now have to say yes. But in sales, not everything is always logical. Sales conversations can often follow very winding paths.

Either way, you may find out another reason that is keeping the customer from buying with this demand. Possibly one that your customer didn't want to tell you, but now that you're creating some pressure, has to come out with it. Ultimately, it's another objection that you need to take care of in some way. After all, there are plenty of variations on this in this book.

Step 6 - Solve objection

Assuming your customer answered yes to the hypothetical closing question in step 5, then you have sold something ... if you can resolve the objection to the customer's satisfaction. So the close is no longer in the customer's hands, but only in yours. Your customer has already agreed.

Suppose you can resolve it (and only then should you use this method). In that case, you can send the customer an order confirmation directly or ask them to check out - depending on what sales situation you are in and what is common practice at your company.

Together to the goal

This variant is suitable for all those cases where your customer is not the sole decision-maker. This can be the case in B2B as well as in B2C business. Often, when it comes to larger purchase decisions and larger sums, several (co-)decision-makers are involved, not all of whom make the actual decision. Some of them are only influencers, but they still have an important say.

Objections that you often hear in such cases are, for example:

- *"I can't decide that (on my own)."*

- *"That's up to our CEO to decide."*

- *"I'll have to ask my wife (husband) about that first."*

This means that you cannot resolve this issue solely with your interlocutor. Especially if the latter is subject to predetermined decision-making rules. However, this does not preclude you from taking a positive step forward. The goal in this situation is to obtain at least your interlocutor's agreement. And you do that with the following hypothetical question:

- *"Assuming you could decide this on your own, would you accept our offer?"*

- *"Just assuming it was your decision, what would your decision be?"*

Again, there are two possible answers. Either your counterpart says that he would decide in favor of your offer or not. If not, then you need to ask why not and bring the underlying objections to light.

If he would decide in your favor, then you are one step further. You are now in the same boat, so to speak, and together you can make a plan on how to succeed in winning the other decision-makers over to your cause.

Appropriate questions for this might be something like:

- *"And how can we convince your CEO?"*

- *"How can I help you bring the project to a positive decision internally?*

- *"How can we work together to get your wife as excited as you are?"*

- *"Then we should talk to your boss together. When can we do that?"* (If you want to be a little brisker).

The game with the ego

For some products and industries - especially those in the higher-priced or luxury range - you can also go on the counterattack by playing on the customer's ego.

- Customer: *"But that's quite expensive."*
  Salesman: *"That's right. Just right for you, I thought."*
  Of course, that's a bit cheeky and has to be used with a lot of tact.

- Customer: *"That's taking a long time."*
  Salesperson: *"That's why I only put up with this kind of thing from customers like you, where I have the impression that you have the stamina to wait for the really valuable things."*
  Here you combine a praise with a reinterpretation (long duration means it is a valuable product).

- Customer: *"I'm not sure if I really need this equipment."*
  Salesperson: *"We'd be happy to check again. I just thought it was important to you that your unit was not worse equipped than your neighbor's."*

(This is actually an important selling point, for example, for agricultural machinery such as tractors).

A negative game with the ego would also be conceivable. This is riskier, but all the more effective if it works.

- Customer: *"I don't think I need this partial service."*
  Seller: *"We're happy to take those out. I just thought you wanted the highest level of security for your family should something happen to you."*
  If the customer sticks with his objection, he's choosing not to have maximum security for his loved ones. If that's not how you want to argue, then I completely understand. It's borderline morally and relatively dangerous for the relationship level.

All in all, you add a number of exciting facets to your objection handling repertoire when you include your customer's ego.

Basic idea 4: Role reversal

The traditional role distribution in the "objection game" is that the customer raises objections to the seller's offer, and it is the seller's responsibility to refute or resolve them. This is exactly what happens in the vast majority of cases.

But does this have to be the case? Isn't it also possible to break through this classic plot and even turn it around? What if the customer and the salesperson switched roles - at least temporarily? Breaking out of one's usual thought patterns can always lead to new, sometimes very exciting and effective ideas and strategies.

If one considers a role reversal between customer and salesperson, the following variants are conceivable and can be observed in sales practice:

- **The salesperson brings the objection instead of the customer and handles it himself.**
  This is the classic objection anticipation, which we have already discussed in detail in one of the earlier sections.

In the other two variants, the objection is handled by the customer - regardless of who brings it up:

- **The seller brings the objection and the customer deals with it.**

- **The customer brings the objection and deals with it himself.**

The following questions typically come to mind:

- Why would the seller allow this?

- Why should the customer do that?

- How can the salesperson get the customer to take over the objection handling?

With this approach, the advantages for the seller are obvious.

- It means less "argument work" for the salesperson when the customer handles the objection.

- The customer may come up with arguments that invalidate his own objection that the salesperson would not have thought of.

- The arguments that the customer himself brings are more credible for him than those of the seller.

You see, there is a lot to be said about this approach. But how do you get the customer to torpedo his own objections and switch roles with you - temporarily? In the following variants of directly or indirectly inviting the customer to swap roles, you will recognize one or the other communication tool.

"Anything you can say, you also can ask."

The basic pattern, which can be found in virtually all of the variants described, is that of passing the ball back to the customer by means of an appropriate question and thus handing over the role of objection handler to him. According to the motto: *"Everything you can say, you can also ask.*

- *"Why is our proposal nevertheless interesting for you?"*

  The salesperson assumes that the customer is interested (pre-assumption) and asks only for the reasons for this, which at the same time serve as arguments to weaken or outweigh the customer's own objection.

- Customer: *"That's pretty heavy, though."*

  Seller: *"True, it's not the lightest. Why do you think many of our customers buy it anyway?"*

  For starters, offer no resistance and openly admit that it is as the customer claims. In doing so, you reframe the customer's statement "heavy" and replace the word with a not-quite-as-bad-sounding "not the easiest thing to do." In the second sentence, you also use social proof by saying that many of your customers choose the product.

- *"This model is the one with the highest scores in terms of customer satisfaction. Why do you think that is?"*

  Again, you bring social proof into play with the statement about customer satisfaction. With the second sentence, you reinforce the assertion again by incorporating it into a question ... and thus "is it so!"

- *"If you decided against our offer, what would you have to do without?"*

  With this hypothetical question, you literally force the customer to pause for thought. He has to think twice around the corner. Not only does he have to make the objection, you also put him in the scenario where he decides to choose a different offer.

- Salesperson: *"Have you had this objection with any of your previous purchases?"*
  Customer: *"Yes."*
  Salesperson: *"And why did you decide to do it anyway?"*

Here you try to convince the customer with his own behavior. He had the objection and bought anyway. You have now caught him in the act. The customer thus goes from being the aggressor to being the defender. The reasons for this can be quite revealing.

- *"You already had these concerns, I assume, before our conversation today. Why did you want to have it anyway?"*
  The presumption is: Now that you're here, you're interested.

- *"And what do you think I should do now?"* or *"And what would you do in my place?"*
  With this very direct way of asking the customer to switch roles, you literally force him to put himself in your shoes as a salesperson.

In order for the role reversal method to succeed in your sales practice, one fundamental point is crucial: you have to stop yourself from slipping quite automatically into the ancestral role of the person who argues against the customer's objections. The point is to switch off this impulse and not react as if pressing a button and making a counter-argument.

As you can see, I'm repeating myself. But I must confess: I'm not even sorry. Since this is perhaps the most important basic idea of the whole book and on the subject of objection handling in general, I want to be sure that every reader has really noticed it and understood its meaning.

Basic idea 5: Arguing and balancing

The last basic idea for dealing with objections deals - at least to some extent - with classic argumentation or counter-argumentation. If you want to go down this path, then you should at least go down it in such a way that you can progress quickly and safely along it.

Argumentation

Therefore, the first thing we should consider is typical argument/counter argumentation. As mentioned at the beginning, counter argumentation harbors the danger that both - seller and customer - bury themselves deeper and deeper in their own positions, from which they can no longer get out without losing face. A solution or agreement thus becomes a distant prospect.

And yet there is a little communicative trick you can use to make counterarguments easier to digest and to take away some of their harshness or sharpness. This is where the little word "And" comes into play, which we have already encountered in an earlier post.

- Customer: *"But the sales are a bit high, I think."*
  Seller: *"Yes, **but** it's just in line with the current fashion."*
  Seller: *"Yes, **and** it is exactly in line with the current fashion."*

Let both variants have an effect on you. Do you notice the difference? Do you feel it? In the first, not recommended variant (therefore crossed out), the salesperson works with a "Yes, but ...". The yes is only a "pseudo agreement". He does not really agree with the customer. Rather, he goes into resistance and brings a justification for the amount of the sale. In doing so, he weakens his negotiating position. He becomes the defender. He goes one better and says "Take it or leave it, that's just the way it is!" without saying it.

"BUT separates, AND connects."

In the second variant, he formulates his statement with a "Yes, and ..." instead of a "Yes, but ...". This transforms the yes in its meaning. It becomes a real agreement. The AND combines this agreement with an argument that forms a positive counterweight to the high paragraph: It's hot right now, in fashion. The customer can now weigh up for himself whether he will accept the higher sales in exchange for being fashionably ahead. The temptation is great ... I think.

One more thing. Earlier in the book, we looked at a positive variant of the "Yes, but ...". The difference to this one is that there the yes was not limited to a yes, but was a comprehensive admission of negative arguments and thus honest and credible.

Replace your BUTs with ANDs. You will be amazed how often and also how well this works. The only difficult part is - once again - to switch off the automatism that produces the "Yes, but ...". We use the but in very many situations where it is not necessary at all:

- *"I wanted to go on vacation, but **and** I couldn't."*

- *"Yesterday we went out, but **and** managed to get to bed before midnight."*

Now, admittedly, there is nothing at all against using the but in cases like these. I just wanted to point out to you how often we use it in everyday language but and that it is not necessary because it could be replaced by and. This frequent use is, in my opinion, why it sits so deeply and sometimes causes us problems in sales.

The request: "Don't use the 'Yes, but ...' at all anymore!" I think is exaggerated. Instead, my advice is to use it where you want to use it consciously and intentionally. Where you might want to go into conscious resistance and separate. However, in most sales situations, this is not advised.

Weighing

Equipped in this way with the "And" as an instrument, you can now set about putting your positive arguments into the field. Weighing for objection follows the basic idea that everything in life has advantages and disadvantages. You, too, have not yet bought anything that had only advantages. After all, you paid the price for it, which I would definitely consider a disadvantage. Nevertheless, that didn't stop you from buying it.

Your customers feel the same way. They mentally put the advantages on one scale and the disadvantages on the other. Ultimately, they buy when the advantages outweigh the disadvantages. This can sometimes produce strange outgrowths. For example, I bought a suit that looked great and was a real bargain, but simply didn't fit. I knew it when I tried it on, but I didn't want to admit it because the benefits were so great. The moral of the story is that I never wore it and eventually gave it away. Have you experienced anything similar?

Such and similar examples demonstrate how we frequently act irrationally and unreasonably when making decisions. They also demonstrate that even significant disadvantages can be outweighed by appropriate advantages.

It is now a matter of filling the scales with as many as possible, but most importantly, the right arguments that speak in favor of your offer. But what are the appropriate arguments? The answer could fill entire books, but in a nutshell, the right arguments are those that are correct in the customer's eyes. According to the motto:

"The bait must taste good to the fish,
not the angler."

For our image with the scales, this means that the right arguments simply weigh much more heavily than any. The wrong ones can not only be lightweights, but in some cases, even counterproductive. You can find out what the right arguments are by conducting a detailed needs assessment and asking the appropriate questions:

- *"What is most important to you when it comes to buying your new vehicle?"*

- *"What is important to you about this project?"*

- *"When you decide to use an external service provider, what criteria are particularly relevant to you?"*

To deal with objections, you can then compare the advantages and disadvantages on a sheet of paper, as I explained in the topic "Comparison of competitors". The goal is to list so many and such weighty advantages that even major objections are compensated for and the customer buys despite them.

Arguing with examples

But arguments don't always have to be so rational and factual. It doesn't have to be the list of criteria I just mentioned every time. Quite the opposite. Manage to appeal not (only) to the mind, but also to the emotions, and to generate helpful emotions in the customer with your arguments. You will significantly improve your chances of closing the deal. And this works very well with stories, examples and comparisons.

Testimonials - stories and examples from other customers

Tell the story of another customer who had the same objection, then choose your offer anyway and never regretted his decision. It's even better if they tell their story themselves - the classic testimonial strategy. There are several ways to do this:

- Establish a rapport between your new customer and the existing, satisfied customer. This sounds a bit elaborate, but it's a common approach for major purchases or projects.

- Have your satisfied customers write statements that address exactly the relevant objections and present or send them to the customer during the conversation. Or have them saved on your website and the customer can read them there.

- If you've videotaped your satisfied customer's statement rebutting the exact objection at issue, that's even more compelling.

When making customer statements, make sure that they are ideally

- formulated very specifically - to a particular point or objection,

- labelled with name, profession or place (depending on the type of offer) and

- are supplemented with a photo or even, as mentioned, with a video.

Of course, as a salesperson, you could also be a customer because you use the product yourself and tell your own story about the product. This is definitely helpful, but the statements of other customers are more credible.

General stories

But even stories and examples that have nothing at all to do with your product or service can be useful when it comes to overcoming objections. For example, you can present a customer who raises a price objection with the front page of a current newspaper with the headline "Everything is getting more expensive" in big bold letters (of course, only if the objection is not about a comparison to a cheaper competitor's product).

Which stories and examples these can be depends, of course, very much on the content of the objection. I have collected even more suitable examples for price objections in the - already mentioned - book "Price Objection Handling Made Easy – 118 proven sales tactics, that never leave you speechless in a price negotiation". >> https://amzn.to/3RGSREe

While reading the last few paragraphs, you may have already wondered where to get all these stories, examples, or even comparisons. That's a good question. One thing in advance: They probably won't come to you spontaneously in the heat of the moment when you need them and may be a bit nervous anyway.

If you want to work with stories and examples to deal with objections, this will only work if you prepare them. Consider which examples correspond to which objections and, ideally, develop a suitable story or a coherent statement of a testimonial for each objection that arises more frequently. If you consistently collect these, you will have a well-stocked fund over time. Very experienced salespeople seem to be able to come up with the right stories quite easily. Not necessarily because they are so brilliant, but because they have filled their fund over time.

Compare

We have already worked with comparisons in the context of competitor comparisons. But it doesn't necessarily have to be the competition that is being compared to. If it serves your purposes and underpins your statements, makes them more effective and more memorable, you can make comparisons of literally all kinds. Often a comparison - because it is usually more pictorial - is worth a thousand words.

Verbal comparisons

The most common variant of comparison is verbal comparison - i.e. you put your comparison into words. The classic "The Mercedes among the ..." is quite worn out (therefore, I would not recommend it anymore), but it underlines what I want to say. Mercedes is known and whether you like Mercedes or not, Mercedes stands in any case for a certain luxury and German quality work. Of course, it's better to bring in BMW, Audi, or even Maserati (to stay with cars) if you know that your customer prefers these brands and you fit your offer.

Even suitable comparisons will not normally fly to you in a sales talk if you urgently need them. If you want to use them, you have to prepare them ... like many other things in this context.

How do you come up with matching comparisons? Ask yourself:

- On what kind of objection do you want to argue?
    - Price

- o Quality
- o Weight
- o Speed
- o Longevity/durability
- o Service orientation
- o Innovation
- o Security
- o Stability of value
- o etc.

- In terms of such objections, which well-known branded product or branded company has a good name and somehow fits your offer? But it could also be something completely different. If you are about speed, for example, ask yourself: What is fast?

- Does the selected comparison also fit into the world of your customer?

A few examples of this:

- *"With us, your money is as safe as in Fort Knox."* (Objection: Security)

- *"The airbag for your portfolio in the event of a stock market crash."* (Objection: Security)

- *"This is the Tesla of televisions."* (Objection: Innovation)

- *"You'll sleep like a baby on this mattress."*

Or else:

- Customer: *" But the device is quite heavy."*
  Seller: *"It has 3.5 kilograms. That's about half the weight of an average vacuum cleaner."*

- Customer: *"But it's taking a long time to deliver."*
  Salesman: *"Look at this watch here, I've been waiting a full six years for this one."*

A former colleague of mine actually had this happen to him with a steel Rolex. With this comparison is also communicated: You have to wait longer for the really valuable things and it is also worth it.

The comparison can also be a "double" one. A few examples of this:

- *"Calling a Tesla a car is like saying an iPhone is a phone."*

- *"To say our products are durable would be like calling a diamond a stone."*

- *"If you would just call our service good, then the Burj Khalifa is just a tall building."*

The possibilities for drawing comparisons are almost inexhaustible. With all the examples I can bring here, therefore, only a very small section is covered. Perhaps something like a window in the aforementioned Burj Khalifa. For the really good and suitable ideas, you need to think on the basis of your concrete offer.

Graphical comparisons

Transform your product or service presentations with engaging visuals! Graphical comparisons can be especially powerful in showcasing size ratios, lengths, surface structures, and other similar aspects of your offerings. Impress your customers with quick, hand-drawn sketches that don't need to be perfect, but still effectively convey your message. This technique is known as "Pencil Selling." Alternatively, you can use a pre-prepared graphic that's either printed out or easily accessible in digital form.

Break down

For some objections - especially price objections - it can be helpful to break down numbers to use as an argument. An example of this:

- Customer: *"But the shoes are quite expensive."* Salesman: *"That's right, 400 euros is an investment. If you wear them, like the ones you're wearing right now, for ten years - which I'm sure will be the case - that's about 77 cents a week. For a single coffee, you'll spend four times that amount every day."*

Breaking it down first and then comparing it - even to something completely different that the customer owns or consumes - is effective.

DEALING WITH YOUR OBJECTIONS

This book was designed to provide you with a comprehensive yet brief overview of the most effective strategies for handling your customers' objections. Our goal is not to exhaustively cover every possible scenario, but rather to equip you with the most important and practical techniques that will make your sales experience smoother and more successful. We believe we have accomplished that and hope this guide serves as a valuable resource for you in your sales journey.

But, as is always the case with paper (or bits if you read the book as an e-book), paper is very patient. If you truly want to enjoy the benefits it brings to your sales conversations, as well as expand or realize the potential it holds, do the following:

- Work through the book again.

- Highlight the methods and strategies that are a particularly good fit for you or your business.

- Based on this, create concrete variants that you can use 1:1 in your sales talks.

- Practice them. Make sure you have internalized them so well that you can apply them with ease in your sales conversations.

If you do, I promise you that the price you paid for this book will pay off for your hundreds or even thousands of times over

- in the form of better customer relationships, more and faster deals, and higher contribution margins, earnings, or fees.

I wish you every success in this endeavor.

ABOUT THE AUTHOR

Meet Roman Kmenta, a marketing and pricing guru with over three decades of international expertise as an entrepreneur, keynote speaker, and bestselling author. Roman leverages his extensive experience in marketing and sales across B2B and B2C sectors to help over 100 of the top companies in Germany, Switzerland, and Austria, as well as countless small businesses and individual entrepreneurs.

His impact is far-reaching, with over 25,000 monthly readers of his weekly blog and listeners of his podcast. Roman provides inspiring insights on the topic of "profitable growth" for salespeople, executives, and entrepreneurs alike, advocating for a value-driven approach to sales and marketing. Get ready to be motivated and empowered by his thought-provoking talks.

www.romankmenta.com

Photo: Matern, Vienna

Perfect for international sales organizations

1 book in 23 languages

For more information:
https://www.romankmenta.com/buch-zu-teuer-international

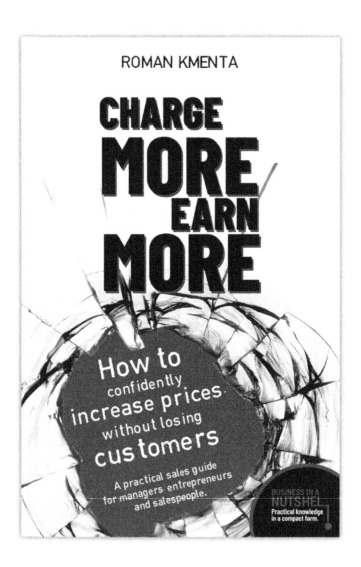

Charge more earn more

Top strategies to enforce higher prices!

Achieving higher prices is a key success factor for most companies. A very special challenge is to carry out price increases with existing customers in such a way that the customer remains a customer. It is important to know about and implement a number of decisive strategies in sales and marketing.

This book is dedicated to these strategies. Pricing and price increases are issues that affect the entire company. Roman Kmenta 84 Accordingly, some of the recommended approaches are comprehensive, far-reaching, and in-depth. At the same time, you will also find tips in this book that can be implemented quickly and easily, which will make the next price increase easier and bring you a lot of money.

In this book, you will learn:

- when the optimal time is for a price increase
- how not to make a price increase look like one
- how to avoid price comparability
- how to increase the value of your offer in the eyes of the customer
- how to avoid price negotiations
- which price psychological affects you should be aware of
- which arguments you can use to support a price increase
- how to raise prices without raising prices.

Higher prices, higher contribution margins, and more income.

A book that pays off.

www.romankmenta.com/shop

ROMAN KMENTA

HOW TO
WRITE OFFERS
THAT SELL

44
psychological
strategies to create
a successful offer

A practical sales guide for
managers, entrepreneurs
and salespeople

BUSINESS IN A
NUTSHEL
Practical knowledge
in a compact form.

How to write offers that sell

44 psychological strategies to create a successful offer!

Written offers are a greatly underestimated instrument in the sales process. A lot of companies produce many of them, but pay little attention to them. Offers are silent salespeople, who spend more time with or at the customer, than the sales force in some business areas and industries.

So how can you raise the potential that lurks in your offers and turn them into better sellers? How can you design your offers to convince your customers?

In this book you will learn

- why your customers basically don't care about your offer and what they are really interested in
- how to build up offers effectively in terms of sales psychology
- how your offers can be made much more attractive with the right design
- what the most promising ways of delivering your offers are
- which price psychological strategies you use to make your offers appear more favorable
- how you clearly differentiate yourself from your competitors through your offers
- what a "Shock and Awe Package" is and how you can use it in a targeted manner.

Better offers bring more sales to a close.

A book that pays off.

www.romankmenta.com/shop

The Keynote Speech for your next Event

"Not at any Price -
A Plea for Value in Times of Cheapness"

Keynote Speaker Roman Kmenta will bring motivation to executives, entrepreneurs, salespeople and distributors at your next event.

For bookings please contact:
service@romankmenta.com
www.romankmenta.com

Printed in Great Britain
by Amazon